Boat, Dive & Fish Catalina Island

By

Bruce Wicklund

Published by

Black Dolphin Diving

Catalina Island, California

2005

Boat, Dive & Fish Catalina Island

Published by
Black Dolphin Diving
5022 Two Harbors,
Avalon, California 90704.
www.divecatalina.com

International Standard Book Number 0-9646281-5-5

Printed in the United States of America by
Southern California Graphics, Culver City, California

Special thanks to:

Cindy Spring
Jim Morrow
Susie Regeimbal
Paul Wintler
Steve and Diana Madaras
Carol and Rainer Lorch
Scott Costa
Greg Warner
Curt Cameron
Dave Carpenter
The Cherry Cove Out to Lunch Bunch
Santa Catalina Island Company

Cover

50 lb 10 oz halibut caught by Harley Osborne aboard his sportfisher "Jocko"
Largest halibut ever caught in Catalina Harbor and posibly the whole Island.
Caught on a large sardine at 3:15 PM on October 1, 2004.

Color photos by:

David Erwitt, Dave Lieberman and Ernesto Rodriguez

TABLE OF CONTENTS

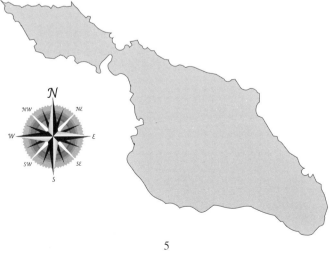

PREFACE

Boat, Dive & Fish Catalina Island has evolved over the years. Originaly the *Guide to Diving Catalina Island (1995)* was expanded to *Boating and Diving Catalina Island (2000)*. This new book is a field guide of useful information for boaters, divers and fishermen visiting Catalina Island. Simple, common names and places familiar to Islanders are used. The drawings of Catalina and various harbors, coves and sites are for general reference and are not intended for use in navigation. Although not to scale, the location drawings combine aerial photos, GPS coordinates, moorings, fish icons, suggested anchoring and general reef layout.

Catalina Island is the premiere destination for boaters in Southern California. Numerous yacht clubs maintain facilities here. Many boaters in one area can be a problem. Mooring or anchoring on a busy weekend can cause confusion. Try to maintain a safe and courteous attitude. Watch your wake (even on open waters)! There are many services to help you. We are all here to enjoy ourselves.

Many divers visit Catalina every year, so common sense and safety are important. Spearfishing, caves, wrecks and deep diving sites mentioned in the various locations may require special skills and training before diving. Divers are responsible for using safe diving procedures within personal limitations. Hopefully the information and opinions provided will enhance the enjoyment and safety of diving at Catalina Island and provide a good start toward planning a dive.

Fishermen will find general information on fishing locations, techniques, cleaning and recipies. Fishermen are secretive about thier favorite spots, but information on fish habitats and icons on the site pages will help you get started. The fishing techniques and rigs are used my many of the best local fishermen. Good luck!

When fishing or hunting game, observe all Fish and Game rules and regulations. These rules are constantly changing and you are responsible for knowing them. Be aware of special closed areas and marine preserves. Pay attention to special tools, measuring devices, size and bag limits. Divers should read the Fish & Game section on invertebrates before taking lobster and scallops. Always practice conservation

This book is written as a field guide to keep onboard and use. Following a dive or fishing trip, use the book to log in your specific observations and other information for future reference. I hope it helps you fully enjoy this enchanting Island.

I. CATALINA INFORMATION

General information, geography, history, and
shipwrecks of Catalina Island.

INTRODUCTION TO CATALINA

Santa Catalina Island was formed long ago by colliding earth plates and volcanic activity. Originally all the channel islands and Mexico's Coronados and Todos Santos were connected and located off the coast of Mexico. Catalina is slowly moving up the California coast a little over 1/2 inch per year. The island is 21.7 miles long, 7.5 miles across at its widest point and covers an area of 75 square miles. Mount Orizaba is the highest peak (2097') and Black Jack Mountain (2006') is second. The temperate climate is similar to mainland beach communities with an average temperature of 55°F in the winter to 65°F in the summer. Prevailing west winds may change to northeast (Santana) from October to early spring. The rainy season extends from mid October to early April and averages about 13 inches per year. Catalina Island is the second largest of the eight Channel Islands and the only island with a year-round resident population.

Catalina Island is a popular resort, due to its Mediterranean-like climate and atmosphere and its proximity to southern California (only 19 miles), over a million people visit annually. Boaters can use moorings or anchor around the island. Cross channel carriers frequent Two Harbors and Avalon. Numerous activities are available including snorkeling, diving, boating, hiking, bicycling, horseback riding, golf, tennis, fishing, kayaking, parasailing, shopping and fine dining. Overnight accommodations are available in hotels or vacation rentals or you can camp at several interior campgrounds and boat-in camp sites. For divers, 54 miles of rugged coastline provides sheer drops, reefs, pinnacles, caves, lush kelp beds and abundant marine life. Waters are clear and visibility may exceed 80 feet, although summer plankton blooms may decrease visibility. Water temperature ranges from 64°F to 74°F degrees in the summer and 54°F to 59°F degrees in winter.

Over 500 species of plants and animals inhabit Catalina Island. Some are Catalina endemic natives; that is they exist here and nowhere else in the world. (Examples: Catalina Ironwood, Catalina fox, Catalina quail) Other Catalina natives can be found elsewhere, either on the mainland or on other Channel Islands (ex: bald eagle, prickly pear cactus, ravens). The ocean buffers the climatic extremes experienced on the mainland. Catalina's rugged and varied topography and buffered marine climate offers specialized niches for Catalina's plants and animals to survive. Many plants and animals have been introduced and are not native to the island. For example, fourteen buffalo, or more correctly, North American bison, were introduced in 1924 for the filming of a Zane Grey movie and their descendants are still here. Today, the herd is maintained at around 150 head. Other introduced plants and animals have proven to be threatening to the island. For example, the non-native feral goats caused massive erosion damage before they were controlled. The island is especially beautiful in the spring when the green hills are painted with wildflowers. For information about ways to access Catalina's interior, (hiking, biking, camping, bus trips) visit the Visitors Bureau in Avalon, Visitor Services in Two Harbors and the Santa Catalina Island Conservancy.

ISLAND HISTORY

At least 7,000 years ago, a group of hunter/gatherers naturally migrated to the island. The largest communities of these "Native Islanders" were located at Emerald Bay, Two Harbors, Little Harbor and Avalon (Bay of the Moon), plus about 40 smaller villages. The early natives called the island Pima or Pimugna and they were referred to as the Pimu or Pimugnans (people of the gray whale). Ravens and rattlesnakes were sacred. Their culture was based on the sea and trade. They traveled to the mainland and other islands in redwood planked canoes (ti'ats). Some items of trade were soapstone (steatite) and cooking bowls (ollas) which could withstand heat without cracking. The Pimu developed a thriving soapstone industry at Empire Landing, whose artifacts remain. Juan Rodriguez Cabrillo discovered the island for Spain in 1542 and named it San Salvador for his flagship. Sixty years later, Vizcaino rediscovered the island and named it Santa Catalina in honor of the martyr Saint Catherine of Alexandria. In the late 1700's, Aleut and Kodiak Indians were brought in by Russian fur traders to hunt the sea otters. Outside contact brought disease, which decimated the local native population. The last Native Islanders were removed in the early 1800's to the San Gabriel Mission and are referred to as Gabrielinos. After the War of 1812, smugglers used the Island to stash goods to avoid paying duty. In 1823, Samuel Prentiss rowed to Emerald Bay with a crude map, given him by Chief Turei, showing treasure buried by white pirates. He built a cabin there becoming one of the first Americans to settle. In 1846, the last Mexican Governor of California, Don Pio Pico, was rumored to have granted the title to Catalina to Thomas Robbins in trade for a fresh horse and a silver saddle during his final retreat to Mexico. When the Mexican American War ended in 1848, California and the Channel Islands became part of American territory. George Yount (sea otter hunter) was rumored to have found gold on the North End of Catalina or San Clemente Island which began a mining boom in the 1840's. In 1854, Santos Bouchette, told by a dying Prentiss of the treasure, searched and later discovered silver at Cherry Valley. He and his wife settled at Johnson's Landing (Emerald Bay). They built a boarding house for miners and worked mines at Cherry, Fourth of July, Emerald, and Parson's. By 1876, the mines were no longer profitable and Bouchette loaded his possesions and sailed away. Numerous mines were dug throughout the Island. A large operation at Black Jack transported ore to a processing and loading area at White's Cove. The Island was used by smugglers for a variety of goods. Catalina (China Point) was used to hide Asian immigrants when the "China Boy" laws forced deportation.

During the Civil War, from Jan - Sep 1864, 83 men of the Fourth Infantry of California Volunteers (Union) fortified the Isthmus at Two Harbors. The barracks, commandants house and a bunker remain. George Shatto bought the island in 1887 for $200,000, building Avalon as a resort until he ran out of money. In 1892, the Bannings purchased Catalina and formed the Santa Catalina Island Company. They further developed Avalon, built roads across the Island and a house at the Isthmus (Banning House Lodge). The Tuna Club was founded as sportfishing flourished. Most of Avalon was destroyed in 1915 by fire. Finally in 1919, William Wrigley Jr. joined a syndicate to purchase Catalina Island, sight unseen. Upon visiting the island and falling in love with it, he bought the remaining interest. Wrigley developed the island as an affordable vacation destination.

The Island resort boomed. The golf course (oldest in California), Airport-in-the-Sky and famous Casino building (1929) were built. Wrigley's Chicago Cubs held "spring training" here. Yachts and movie stars visited regularly. Large production movies were filmed at Catalina including "Mutiny on the Bounty", "The Black Pirate" and "Old Ironsides." In 1932, Philip K. Wrigley assumed control of the company. During World War II, the military maintained guns and bunkers at Ben Weston Point and training barracks at Camp Cactus. The tugs of the Wilmington Transportation Company (a wholly owned subsidiary of the Santa Catalina Island Company at the time) were painted gray and pressed into service. After the war, visitors returned to the island once again. William Wrigley Jr.'s vision for the future of Catalina Island was that it remain protected for all generations. Therefore, it was fitting when in 1975, his descendants (Wrigley and Offield families) donated 86 percent of the Island (42,135 acres) to form the Santa Catalina Island Conservancy, a non-profit foundation. Today the Conservancy is involved in restoring and preserving Catalina Island's natural environment.

SHIPWRECKS

The island's first inhabitants crossed the channel in plank canoes. Spanish ships traded along the route from Manila to Mexico. Otter hunters and smugglers plied the waters for profit. Yachts traveled to the island resort for relaxation. Many were lost or stranded in storms. Some were accidentally destroyed by fire or torched for a movie scene. Most of the wrecks listed have deteriorated, scattered or disappeared. Researching Catalina shipwreck history is often confusing and misleading. Few remnants remain at the sites. The following general information is composed from several sources.

SPANISH (MANILA) GALLEONS
From 1565 to 1815, the Manila galleons sailed California's waters. Several Spanish galleons and frigates have been reported or rumored to be lost around Catalina Island. Many efforts have been made to locate some of the wrecks, but have thus far been unsuccessful. Possibilities include: **SANTA MARTA:** Struck a rock and was stranded off the West End, Catalina in 1582. Cargo valued at $100,000 to $200 million. Crew and some cargo saved; **SAN PEDRO:** Manila galleon wrecked and sank in 14 fathoms at Arrow Point Reef? Gold and silver cargo worth over $2 million. Wreckage may have washed ashore in 1602 and in 1850 parts of the hull possibly discovered in 6 fathoms at Ship Rock; **NUESTRA SENORA AYUDA:** 300 ton Galleon wrecked on a rock and foundered west of Catalina in 1641 with treasure worth $500,000. Some crew survived but cargo lost; **SAN SEBASTIAN:** Galleon foundered and sank (175' deep) west of Catalina in January 7, 1754. Upon learning that the ship would be carrying treasure from Manilla, pirate "English George" (George Compton) set up a settlement at Catalina and prepared to intercept.The pirate forced the ship aground off the West End. Compton was rumored to have captured and killed the remaining 21 crew and passengers. Gold, silver and oriental treasure may have been burried at Emerald Bay (see pg. 10); **SANTA CECILIA:** Frigate foundered September, 1852, off Ship Rock with cargo valued at $100,000.

1832	**JOSEPHINE:** Wrecked at Catalina.
1890	**ALEUT:** Tug. Ashore on Nov. 12. Total loss and one dead.
1891	**FAWN:** Sloop. Lost in a gale on February 8. Two dead.
1920	**NORTH STAR:** Wrecked at Catalina on November 4.
1924	**TAURUS:** Four masted 551-ton schooner. Built 1902. Burned for a motion picture at Catalina on July 31.
1924	**PROSPER:** Three-masted 241-ton schooner. Built 1892. Burned for a motion picture at Catalina on August 2.
1924	**ALPINE:** 95-ton. Built 1892. Burned at Avalon in October 29.

1926 **WILLIAM G. IRWIN:** 348-ton barkentine. Built 1881.
Burned for a motion picture at Catalina on May 15.

1926 **S. N. CASTLE:** Three masted, 514-ton schooner. Built 1886.
Burned for a motion picture at Catalina on May 15.

1926 **LLEWELLYN J. MORSE:** 1392-ton ship. Built 1877.
Burned at Catalina on September 11. Filmed in the motion
picture "The Black Pirate" and portrayed U.S.F. CONSTITUTION
in the silent movie "Old Ironsides."

1929 **CHARLES F. CROCKER:** 204 ft. long with 40 ft. beam, four
masted, 762 ton barkentine. Built 1890 at Alameda, CA. Blown up
for a movie then beached and later burned at Catalina Harbor (pg. 69).

1930 **VALIANT:** Catalina Island's most famous shipwreck.163 feet long
with 26 ft beam, 444-ton steel motoryacht. Built 1926. One of the
largest private yachts in the world at the time. A gas generator may
have exploded. The ship caught fire and was towed out by the Harbor
Patrol until the anchor dropped. Three days it burned and then sank
off Descanso Beach on December 17 (pg. 25).

Reported loss of $67,000 in jewels. Wreck lies perpendicular to shore,
listing to port, stern in sand at 80 feet and bow at 110 feet deep.

Famous for brass coins with inscription "yacht Valiant / Good for
one drink". Dive permit required from Avalon Harbormaster. Permits
may be denied at times of heavy summer boat traffic.

MORE WRECKS

1931 **WINDWARD:** 63-ton yawl. Built 1907. Burned at Catalina on July 25.

1931 **LADY ALTA:** 102-ton yawl. Built 1930. Burned at Catalina in September.

1932 **ADVANCE:** Three-masted schooner. Sank at Catalina on September 8.

1933 **MARGARET C.:** 69 ft. long with 25 ft. beam, 2 masted 58 ton schooner. Built 1889 in San Francisco. Blown up in 1926 then burned and later beached on May 3 (pg. 69).

1935 **NING PO:** 138 ft. long chinese junk. Built 1753 in Fu Chau, China. Hull constructed of ironwood with teak decks. Carved to resemble a sea monster. Originaly named KIN TAI FOONG, she was the fastest ship in Chinese waters. Notorious and bloody history included piracy, smuggling and slavery. 158 pirates were once beheaded on her deck. Seized by Col. Peter "Chinese" Gordon in 1861 and renamed after the city of Ning Po (Calm Seas). Sailed from Shanghai and arrived in San Pedro in February, 1913, sailing 7,000 miles across the Pacific in 58 days. Towed to Catalina Harbor in 1917. Used in motion pictures, viewed by sight-seers. In 1935, a fire burned her to the waterline, then finally sank at Ballast Point, Catalina Harbor. Remains of the stern, keel and ribs are visible in the mud at low tide. Artifacts on display at the Catalina Island Museum (pg. 69).

The NING PO at Ballast Point, Catalina Harbor.

1937 **KITKA:** U.S. Ship. Lost two miles offshore, on Northwest side of Catalina.

1937 **PRONTO:** Wrecked off Catalina on March 1.

1938 **PALMYRA:** 75 ft. long with 20 ft. beam. Small coastal 2 masted schooner. Built 1876. Posibly used in a movie. Beached and probably burned. Remains of hull visible at low tide (pg. 69).

1941 **RUBY:** Three-masted, 345-ton schooner. Built 1902. Wrecked at Catalina.

1941 **BROTHERS:** 54-ton scow. Built 1890. Foundered at Pebbly Beach on October 10.

1943 **CHICAGO:** 75-ton. Built 1926. Foundered four miles south of Catalina on December 15.

1947 **ROSSINO II:** Wrecked on northwest side of Cat Head, August 22.

1949 **VASHON:** Sank at Catalina in August.

1950 **ONWARD:** 51-ton. Built 1919. Burned 5 miles southwest of Catalina Harbor on February 22. (N33° 22.00' / W117° 45.30').

1952 **BLUE SKY:** 99-ton. Built 1930. Burned 2.5 miles off east end of Catalina on November 17.

1954 **NORTH HEAD:** 50-ton. Burned at Catalina on September 25.

1955 **BENJIE BOY:** 64-ton. Built 1950. Burned 2 miles south of west end of Catalina on April 13.

1956 **GENEVIEVE H. II:** 112-ton. Built 1937. Burned 15 miles southeast of east end of Catalina on Jan. 12.

1956 **SANTA ROSA:** 50-ton steel vessel. Built 1950. Foundered 12 miles southwest of Catalina on November 23.

1960 **WTCO No. 17:** 330-ton barge. Built 1927. Foundered on September 17.

1960 **ZEPHYR:** 104-ton. Built 1938. Burned 5 miles southwest of west end of Catalina Oct. 28.

1966 **OLD TIMER:** 81-ton. Built 1928. Stranded at Avalon, January 17.

1980 **SUJAC:** 54 ft. long ferocement gaff-rigged schooner. Built 1968. Crashed on the Casino Point breakwater and sank during a Northeast storm at Avalon on November 14th. 3 crew were rescued by the harbor patrol. Located at base of southeast buoy in Avalon Underwater Park. Lies on starboard side, bow down, 65 to 90 feet deep, with two holes in the hull (pg.25).

1990 **DIOSA DEL MAR (Goddess of the Sea):** 90 feet long, 60-ton wooden stay sail schooner. Built 1898 in Long Island, NY. Built for the Vanderbilt family and originally named "Unka"after the last Chief of the Mohawk's. Under full sail she truck the wash rocks SE of Ship Rock during the 18th annual Catalina Firemans' Race in July. She sank quickly, in shallow water. Bow section, aluminum masts (wedged in reef) and debris remain. Main wreckage is 25 feet deep and scattered down slope and not much remains (pg. 49).

II. HARBORS, COVES & SITES

Harbors, coves and sites combines aerial photos, navigational aids, moorings, fishing, suggested anchoring, GPS coordinates, general reef area and other information. Circumnavigate the island begining on the frontside at the east end, around the west end, then travel the backside, finally returning to the east end. Use the corners of the pages like flip cards and observe the black dot (indicating map site) move around the Island. See the Catalina fold-out map (back cover) and index of map sites (opposite page) for quick reference.

LEGEND

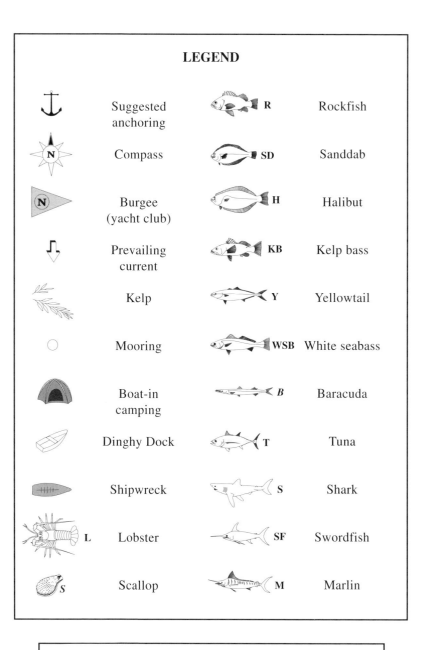

Suggested anchoring	R	Rockfish
Compass	SD	Sanddab
Burgee (yacht club)	H	Halibut
Prevailing current	KB	Kelp bass
Kelp	Y	Yellowtail
Mooring	WSB	White seabass
Boat-in camping	B	Baracuda
Dinghy Dock	T	Tuna
Shipwreck	S	Shark
Lobster	SF	Swordfish
Scallop	M	Marlin

GPS coordinates are from a variety of sources
and may be slightly different from your source.
Course information, GPS and map sites are for reference
only and not for navigational use.

SEAL ROCKS

Seal Rocks: Numerous sea lions. Often poor visibility.
Little America: Sheephead and horn sharks. Keep an eye out for eagles on top of point and along coast.

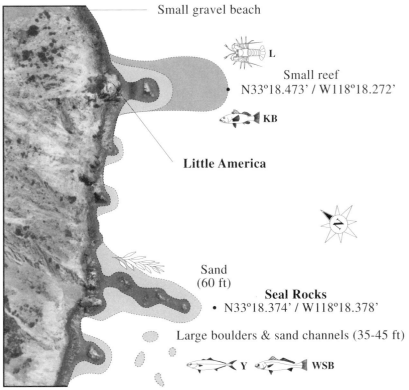

Small gravel beach

L

Small reef
N33°18.473' / W118°18.272'

KB

Little America

Sand
(60 ft)

Seal Rocks
• N33°18.374' / W118°18.378'

Large boulders & sand channels (35-45 ft)

Y **WSB**

○ **East End Light:** N33°18.10' / W118°19.00'; Fl. white 10 sec.; 212 ft. high; Vis. 16 miles, 253° - 068°.

Seal Rocks and Little America looking Southwest.

EAST QUARRY / JEWFISH POINT

East Quarry: In operation since before 1900.
85% of mainland breakwaters built with Catalina rock. **Jewfish Point:** named for a 500 pound black sea bass (now protected) caught there. Ling cod, garibaldi, blue-banded gobi, butterfly fish (in summer) and gorgonians. Mola mola and other pelagics offshore. Beware of boat traffic (tugs and barges), heavy currents and turbid water.

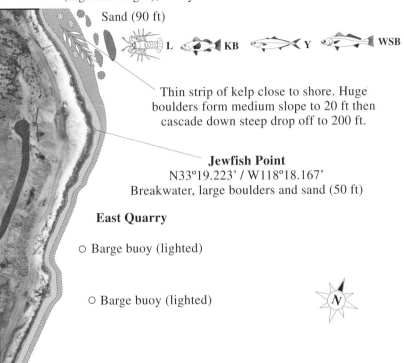

Sand (90 ft)

L   KB   Y   WSB

Thin strip of kelp close to shore. Huge boulders form medium slope to 20 ft then cascade down steep drop off to 200 ft.

Jewfish Point
N33°19.223' / W118°18.167'
Breakwater, large boulders and sand (50 ft)

East Quarry

o Barge buoy (lighted)

o Barge buoy (lighted)

Rock quarry looking West.

LITTLE FARNSWORTH

Also called Pinnacle Rock. Series of rock pinnacles
with peaks and cracks. Located 1 mile east of Avalon and about 75 yards
off point. Boat access only. Depth finder required to locate. Beware of
heavy boat traffic and currents. Divers beware of fish hooks and line (carry
a knife). Black sea bass (protected), sheephead, gorgonians, bat stars,
anemones and nudibranchs .

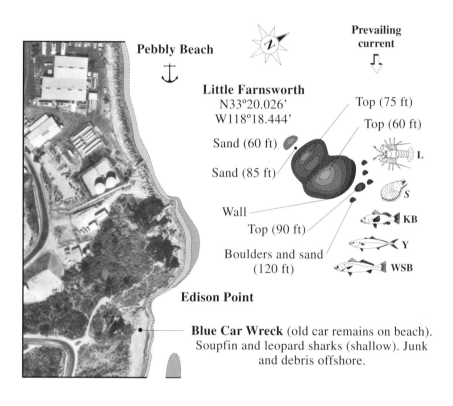

Pebbly Beach

Prevailing
current

Little Farnsworth
N33°20.026'
W118°18.444'

Top (75 ft)

Top (60 ft)

Sand (60 ft)

L

Sand (85 ft)

S

Wall

KB

Top (90 ft)

Y

Boulders and sand
(120 ft)

WSB

Edison Point

Blue Car Wreck (old car remains on beach).
Soupfin and leopard sharks (shallow). Junk
and debris offshore.

From Little Farnsworth looking Southwest to Edison Point.

RING ROCK / LOVERS COVE

Lovers Cove Marine Preserve has numerous
large, friendly fish (bring peas, bread or other fish food). Calico,
sheephead, black sea bass, soupfin shark, leopard shark, garibaldi, opaleye,
treefish, schools of baitfish and starfish. Great snorkeling (NO SCUBA).
Beach entry (no anchoring). Spearfishing is discouraged close to preserve.
Ring Rock marks end of boundary. Beware of boat traffic and boat debris.

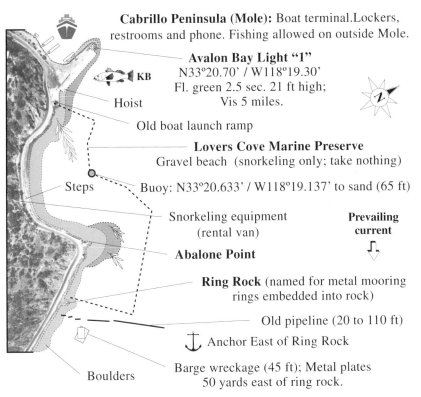

Cabrillo Peninsula (Mole): Boat terminal.Lockers,
restrooms and phone. Fishing allowed on outside Mole.

KB

Hoist

Avalon Bay Light "1"
N33°20.70' / W118°19.30'
Fl. green 2.5 sec. 21 ft high;
Vis 5 miles.

Old boat launch ramp

Lovers Cove Marine Preserve
Gravel beach (snorkeling only; take nothing)

Steps

Buoy: N33°20.633' / W118°19.137' to sand (65 ft)

Snorkeling equipment
(rental van)

**Prevailing
current**

Abalone Point

Ring Rock (named for metal mooring
rings embedded into rock)

Old pipeline (20 to 110 ft)

Anchor East of Ring Rock

Boulders

Barge wreckage (45 ft); Metal plates
50 yards east of ring rock.

Ring Rock and Abalone Point looking West.

CITY OF AVALON (Street Map)

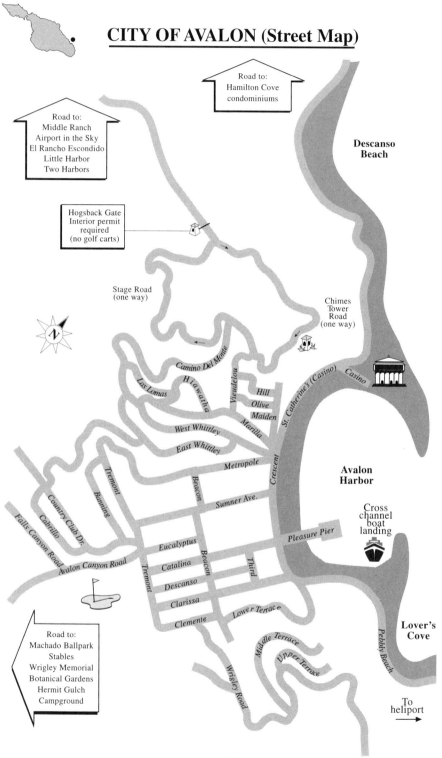

AVALON INFORMATION

Avalon History: Site of a large Native Islander settlement called Bay of the Moon. Known as Timm's Harbor from 1867 to 1887. George Shatto bought the island and re-named it Shatto City. Later renamed Avalon City by Shatto's sister. Incorporated in June 1913 as Los Angeles county's 30th city. Avalon is the only city in the Channel Islands. It covers an area of roughly one square mile and has a population of about 3500. City was completely destroyed by  fire on Nov 29, 1915. USCG and Maritime Service Station during WWII. Resort activity was suspended from 1941 to 1945. Jurisdiction on the water extends from Frog Rock to Pebbly Beach.

Mooring: See Mooring Information on page 80.

Anchoring: East of Ring Rock or west of the red navigation light on the Casino breakwater. 300' outside of moorings. See Anchoring (p.82).

Dinghy Docks: Five, located around harbor. 14 ' maximum length.

Shoreboat: Call for shoreboat on VHF channel 9.

No Discharge Area: To ensure this, the harbor patrol will board and place a green dye tab in the head(s). Strictly enforced. Holding tanks can be emptied at Pump out float or call Head Pumpers on VHF 68.

Floats: Used for loading and unloading only (10 minute limit). Do not leave boat unattended. Keep a spring line ready during surge.

Generators: Secured from 10 PM to 7 AM.

Alcohol: No open containers allowed on streets, pier or floats.

Trash: Free pick up twice daily in summer and on weekends in winter.

Unattended boats: Not allowed. Service may be used to watch boat.

Marine Mechanic: Call Marine Repair on VHF channel 16.

Divers: Call for diving services on VHF channel 12 or contact Harbor Patrol for list of divers.

Fuel: Fuel Dock hours in summer 7 am to 4 pm and in winter, 8 to 10 sam and 2 to 4 pm on weekdays and 8 to 5 pm on weekends.

Propane: Edison Plant, Pebbly Beach (510-0932). Best not to run out.

Water: Available at the pump out float or fuel dock, near the Casino. Please conserve water (washdowns at float not allowed during droughts).

Ice: Available at the shoreboat float, fuel dock and grocery store.

Showers: Pleasure Pier and Casino Way. Hours: Mon - Thu (7am - 11am & 3pm - 6pm). Fri & Sat (7am to 7pm). Sun (7am - 6pm).

Observe 5 mile per hour or wakeless speed in harbor.

AVALON HARBOR

N 33° 20.799' / W 118° 19.321' (Harbor entrance)
See page 79 for mooring information.

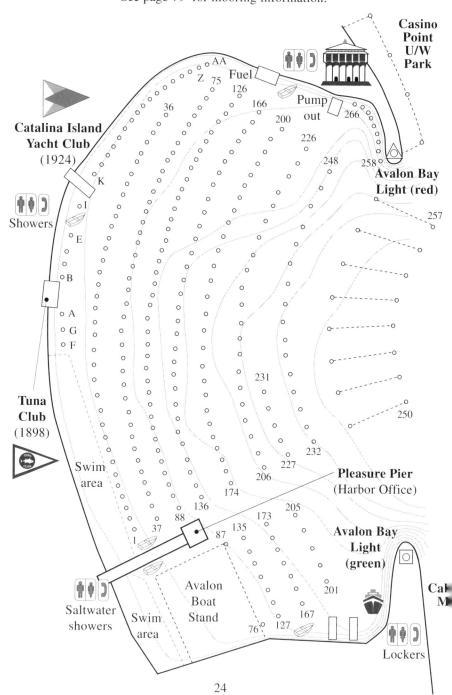

CASINO POINT UNDERWATER PARK

Designed in 1962 by Carl and Maggie Koehler
(past owners of Catalina Divers Supply) and established in 1965. The
underwater park is marked by buoys and rope. Marine preserve (Take
nothing). Numerous fish including kelp bass, sargo, sheephead and kelpfish.
Numerous wrecks (U/W objects may shift positions). Prevailing current is
from the west. Beware of heavy boat traffic when outside of park.

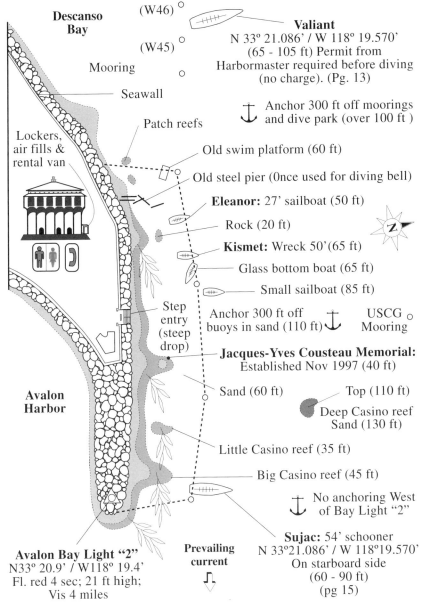

Descanso Bay

(W46)

(W45)

Mooring

Seawall

Patch reefs

Lockers, air fills & rental van

Valiant
N 33° 21.086' / W 118° 19.570'
(65 - 105 ft) Permit from
Harbormaster required before diving
(no charge). (Pg. 13)

Anchor 300 ft off moorings
and dive park (over 100 ft)

Old swim platform (60 ft)

Old steel pier (Once used for diving bell)

Eleanor: 27' sailboat (50 ft)

Rock (20 ft)

Kismet: Wreck 50'(65 ft)

Glass bottom boat (65 ft)

Small sailboat (85 ft)

Step entry (steep drop)

Anchor 300 ft off
buoys in sand (110 ft)

USCG Mooring

Jacques-Yves Cousteau Memorial:
Established Nov 1997 (40 ft)

Avalon Harbor

Sand (60 ft)

Top (110 ft)

Deep Casino reef
Sand (130 ft)

Little Casino reef (35 ft)

Big Casino reef (45 ft)

No anchoring West
of Bay Light "2"

Avalon Bay Light "2"
N33° 20.9' / W118° 19.4'
Fl. red 4 sec; 21 ft high;
Vis 4 miles

Prevailing current

Sujac: 54' schooner
N 33°21.086' / W 118°19.570'
On starboard side
(60 - 90 ft)
(pg 15)

DESCANSO / HAMILTON

All mooring assignments are made at
the main harbor entrance. Anchor minimum of 300' outside
of moorings. Valiant wreck requires a special diving permit which must be
obtained prior to diving the Valiant. Permit available at the Harbor Department
office, free of charge (permit may be denied on busy weekends due to heavy
boat traffic). See page 13 for more information.

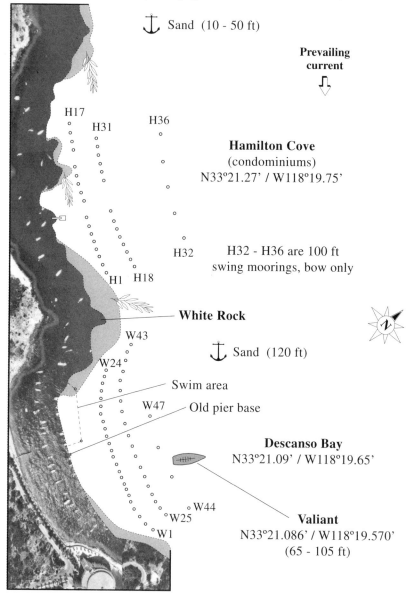

⚓ Sand (10 - 50 ft)

**Prevailing
current**
⇩

H17
H31
H36

Hamilton Cove
(condominiums)
N33°21.27' / W118°19.75'

H32   H32 - H36 are 100 ft
swing moorings, bow only

H1   H18

── **White Rock**

⚓ Sand (120 ft)

W43

W24

── Swim area

W47   ── Old pier base

Descanso Bay
N33°21.09' / W118°19.65'

W44
W25
W1

Valiant
N33°21.086' / W118°19.570'
(65 - 105 ft)

FROG ROCK

Scattered rocks and murky water.
Leopard sharks and bat rays.

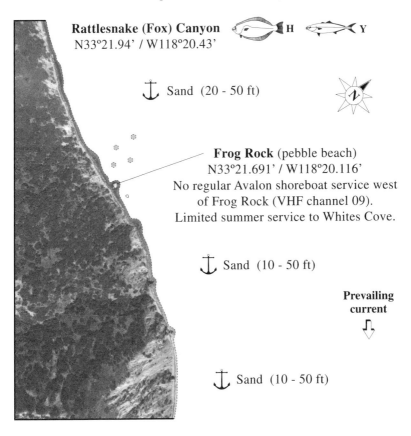

Rattlesnake (Fox) Canyon H   Y
N33°21.94' / W118°20.43'

⚓ Sand (20 - 50 ft)

Frog Rock (pebble beach)
N33°21.691' / W118°20.116'
No regular Avalon shoreboat service west
of Frog Rock (VHF channel 09).
Limited summer service to Whites Cove.

⚓ Sand (10 - 50 ft)

**Prevailing
current**

⚓ Sand (10 - 50 ft)

Frog Rock looking Southwest.

GALLAGHER'S, TOYON
& WILLOW COVE

Willow Cove provides excellent anchorage.
Toyon Bay formerly Swain's Landing. Whittier State Boys School 1893.
Tom **Gallagher's Beach** 1850. Mantis shrimp.

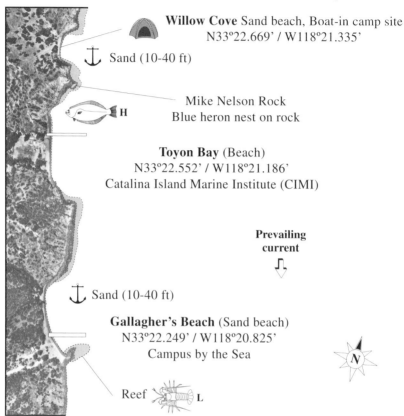

Willow Cove Sand beach, Boat-in camp site
N33°22.669' / W118°21.335'

⚓ Sand (10-40 ft)

Mike Nelson Rock
Blue heron nest on rock

H

Toyon Bay (Beach)
N33°22.552' / W118°21.186'
Catalina Island Marine Institute (CIMI)

**Prevailing
current**

⚓ Sand (10-40 ft)

Gallagher's Beach (Sand beach)
N33°22.249' / W118°20.825'
Campus by the Sea

N

Reef L

Toyon looking West.

TORQUA SPRINGS

Named after Chief Torqua. Horseshoe-shaped reef about 150 yards long. Moderate current. Murky at times. Black sea bass, sheephead, garialdi, blacksmith, senorita, blue banded goby, harbor seal, moray eel, leopard shark (shallow), soupfin shark, bat ray and mantis shrimp (in sand). Former water source for Avalon (large wood tank covered by landslide.

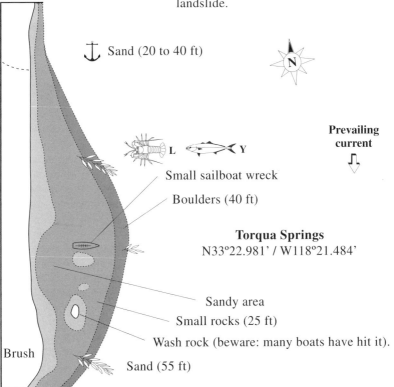

Sand (20 to 40 ft)

N

Prevailing current

L   Y

Small sailboat wreck

Boulders (40 ft)

Torqua Springs
N33°22.981' / W118°21.484'

Sandy area

Small rocks (25 ft)

Wash rock (beware: many boats have hit it).

Brush

Sand (55 ft)

Torqua Springs looking West.

MOONSTONE & WHITE'S

Moonstone Cove: Named for the rounded rocks
on the beach. The cliffs are volcanic. The canyon has good hiking. Bonito.
White's Cove (Landing): Remnants of old silver ore process works and cable
from Blackjack Mine. Former pier at White's was used to load cattle. For
moorings call Moonstone or White's harbor patrol on VHF channel 09.

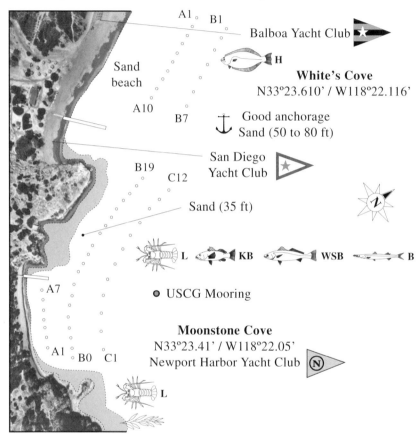

A1 B1

Balboa Yacht Club

H

Sand
beach

White's Cove
N33°23.610' / W118°22.116'

A10

B7

Good anchorage
Sand (50 to 80 ft)

San Diego
Yacht Club

B19

C12

Sand (35 ft)

L KB WSB B

A7

● USCG Mooring

Moonstone Cove
N33°23.41' / W118°22.05'
Newport Harbor Yacht Club

A1 B0 C1

L

Moonstone Cove looking Southwest.

HEN ROCK

Named for large, hen shaped, rock. Hen Rock's reef has large boulders, caves and sand patches. Black sea bass, cabezon, garibaldi, schools of blacksmith, blue-banded gobi, moray eel, horn shark, bat ray, sheep crab, octopus, gorgonians and nudibranchs . Beware of currents and boat traffic. For mooring contact Hen Rock harbor patrol on VHF channel 9.

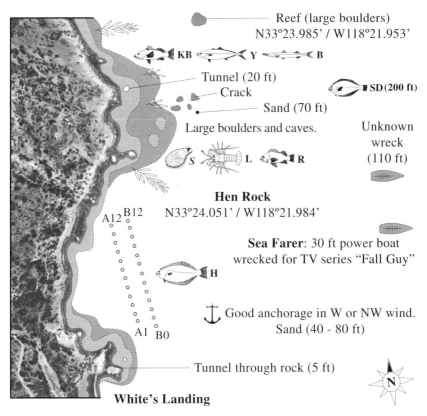

Reef (large boulders)
N33°23.985' / W118°21.953'

KB   Y   B

Tunnel (20 ft)
Crack
Sand (70 ft)
Large boulders and caves.

SD (200 ft)

Unknown
wreck
(110 ft)

S   L   R

Hen Rock
N33°24.051' / W118°21.984'

Sea Farer: 30 ft power boat
wrecked for TV series "Fall Guy"

A12 B12

H

Good anchorage in W or NW wind.
Sand (40 - 80 ft)

A1 B0

Tunnel through rock (5 ft)

N

White's Landing

Hen Rock looking Southwest.

LONG POINT /BUTTONSHELL

Numerous caves. Black sea bass, garibaldi, senorita, blue-banded goby, blacksmith, treefish, squid (spring) and gorgonians. **Pirates Cove:** Good anchorage. Moray eels in boulders. Tunnel (land), viewed from south, is shaped like Catalina. Native Islander's feared the loud whistling sound emitted in strong wind. **Buttonshell:** named for shells found there. "Magic Isle" filmed 1919. For mooring, call Buttonshell harbormaster on VHF 09. Beware heavy currents and boat traffic.

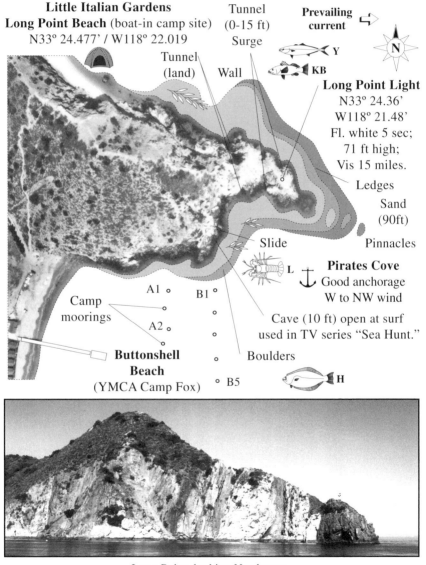

Little Italian Gardens
Long Point Beach (boat-in camp site)
N33° 24.477' / W118° 22.019

Tunnel
(land)

Tunnel
(0-15 ft)
Surge

Wall

Prevailing current

Y

KB

N

Long Point Light
N33° 24.36'
W118° 21.48'
Fl. white 5 sec;
71 ft high;
Vis 15 miles.

Ledges

Sand
(90ft)

Pinnacles

Slide

L

Pirates Cove
Good anchorage
W to NW wind

A1   B1

Camp
moorings

A2

Cave (10 ft) open at surf
used in TV series "Sea Hunt."

Buttonshell Beach
(YMCA Camp Fox)

Boulders

B5

H

Long Point looking Northwest.

32

ITALIAN GARDENS

Named for beaches used by Italian fishermen for
drying nets. Point known to divers as Italian Gardens. Scattered rock piles,
caves, small pinnacles, crevices, cliffs and ledges. Sheephead, moray eel,
horn shark and blue-banded gobi. Beware currents and thick kelp.

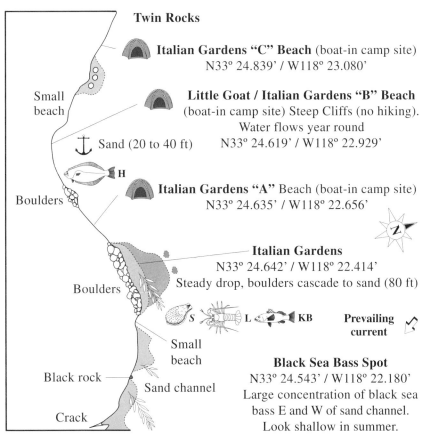

Twin Rocks

Italian Gardens "C" Beach (boat-in camp site)
N33° 24.839' / W118° 23.080'

Small
beach

Little Goat / Italian Gardens "B" Beach
(boat-in camp site) Steep Cliffs (no hiking).
Water flows year round

Sand (20 to 40 ft)   N33° 24.619' / W118° 22.929'

H

Italian Gardens "A" Beach (boat-in camp site)
N33° 24.635' / W118° 22.656'

Boulders

Italian Gardens
N33° 24.642' / W118° 22.414'
Steady drop, boulders cascade to sand (80 ft)

Boulders

S   L   KB   **Prevailing current**

Small
beach

Black rock

Sand channel

Crack

Black Sea Bass Spot
N33° 24.543' / W118° 22.180'
Large concentration of black sea
bass E and W of sand channel.
Look shallow in summer.

Italian Gardens looking South.

TWIN ROCKS / GOAT HARBOR

Goat Harbor once used to land supplies for
Middle Ranch. Nice beach with good anchorage (sand bottom), camping
and hiking (look for eagle and fox). Sheephead, sand bass, blacksmith,
kelpfish, treefish, blue-banded goby, ghost goby, anchovy, angel shark,
leopard shark, guitarfish, bat ray, moray eel, octopus, crabs, spanish shawl,
lemon nudibranch and gorgonians. Beware current off Twin Rocks.

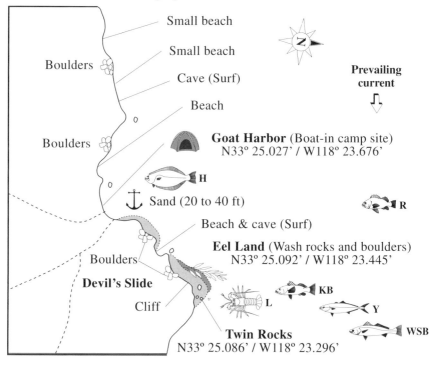

Small beach

Small beach

Boulders

Cave (Surf)

Beach

Goat Harbor (Boat-in camp site)
N33° 25.027' / W118° 23.676'

Boulders

H

Prevailing
current

Sand (20 to 40 ft)

R

Beach & cave (Surf)

Eel Land (Wash rocks and boulders)
N33° 25.092' / W118° 23.445'

Boulders

Devil's Slide

L

KB

Cliff

Y

WSB

Twin Rocks
N33° 25.086' / W118° 23.296'

Twin Rocks looking South.

34

LITTLE GIBRALTAR / CABRILLO

Cabrillo Beach (formerly Steadman's) is a sandy beach, inside Gibraltar Point, with excellent anchorage. Moray eel and octopus.

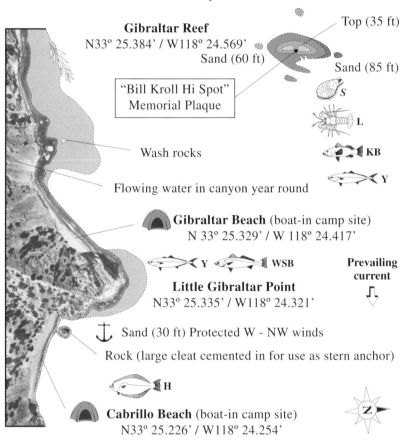

Gibraltar Reef
N33° 25.384' / W118° 24.569'
Sand (60 ft)

Top (35 ft)

Sand (85 ft)

"Bill Kroll Hi Spot"
Memorial Plaque

S

L

Wash rocks

KB

Flowing water in canyon year round

Y

Gibraltar Beach (boat-in camp site)
N 33° 25.329' / W 118° 24.417'

Y   WSB

Prevailing current

Little Gibraltar Point
N33° 25.335' / W118° 24.321'

Sand (30 ft) Protected W - NW winds

Rock (large cleat cemented in for use as stern anchor)

H

Cabrillo Beach (boat-in camp site)
N33° 25.226' / W118° 24.254'

Z

Cabrillo Beach and Little Gibraltar Point looking South.

RED LAVA POINTS

Red lava formations with caves and small reefs.

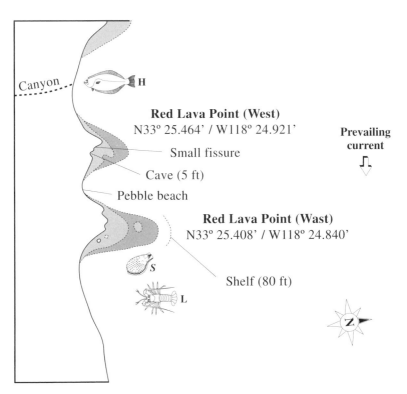

Canyon

H

Red Lava Point (West)
N33° 25.464' / W118° 24.921'

Small fissure

Cave (5 ft)

Pebble beach

Red Lava Point (Wast)
N33° 25.408' / W118° 24.840'

S

Shelf (80 ft)

L

**Prevailing
current**

Z

Red Lava Points looking Southwest.

SEAL POINT / PARADISE COVE

Lava Wall has good anchorage and beach. Eagle nest on cliff. **Seal Point** has harbor seals and sea lions on rocks.

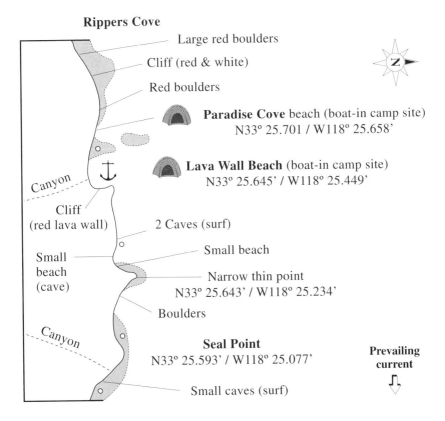

Rippers Cove

Large red boulders

Cliff (red & white)

Red boulders

Paradise Cove beach (boat-in camp site)
N33° 25.701 / W118° 25.658'

Lava Wall Beach (boat-in camp site)
N33° 25.645' / W118° 25.449'

Canyon

Cliff
(red lava wall)

2 Caves (surf)

Small beach

Small
beach
(cave)

Narrow thin point
N33° 25.643' / W118° 25.234'

Boulders

Canyon

Seal Point
N33° 25.593' / W118° 25.077'

**Prevailing
current**

Small caves (surf)

Seal Point looking South.

RIPPER'S COVE / EMPIRE LANDING

Valley of the Ollas (canyon of soapstone bowls), also
called Pott's Valley, is the site of Pimu soapstone industry. In 1602 Viscaino
described an Native Islander temple here. Great hiking. Empire has houses
used by East Quarry workers. Good anchorage. Bat ray and sculpin.

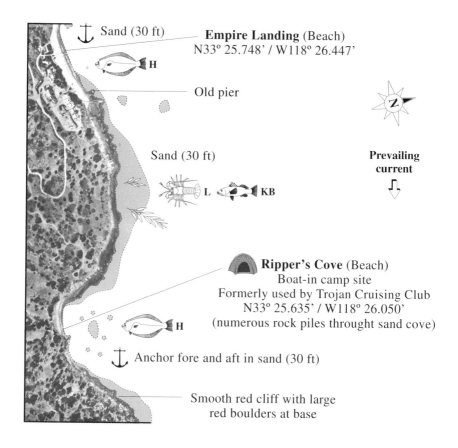

Sand (30 ft)

Empire Landing (Beach)
N33° 25.748' / W118° 26.447'

H

Old pier

Sand (30 ft)

L KB

Prevailing
current

Ripper's Cove (Beach)
Boat-in camp site
Formerly used by Trojan Cruising Club
N33° 25.635' / W118° 26.050'
(numerous rock piles throught sand cove)

H

Anchor fore and aft in sand (30 ft)

Smooth red cliff with large
red boulders at base

Rippers Cove looking Southwest.

38

YELLOWTAIL POINT / WEST QUARRY

Yellowtail Point is shallow and rocky.
West Quarry not in use. Eighty-five percent of mainland breakwaters built with Catalina rock. Moray eel, squid (spring), gorgonians and some bull kelp. Beware of boat traffic and currents.

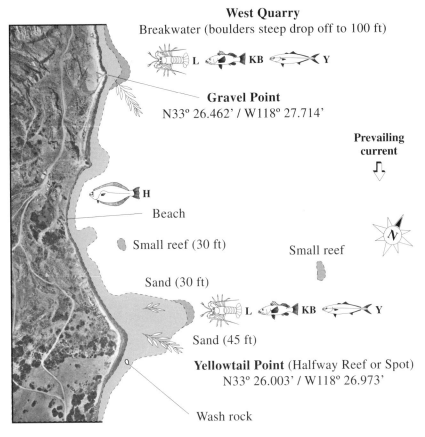

West Quarry
Breakwater (boulders steep drop off to 100 ft)

L   KB   Y

Gravel Point
N33° 26.462' / W118° 27.714'

**Prevailing
current**

H

Beach

Small reef (30 ft)

Small reef

N

Sand (30 ft)

L   KB   Y

Sand (45 ft)

Yellowtail Point (Halfway Reef or Spot)
N33° 26.003' / W118° 26.973'

Wash rock

Yellowtail Point looking Southwest.

SEA FAN GROTTO / CRANE POINT

Sea Fan Grotto is a beautiful dive site, named
for numerous gorgonians. Large lava rock formation at base of white cliff.
Kelpfish, nudibranchs and gorgonians. Beware of boat traffic and currents.

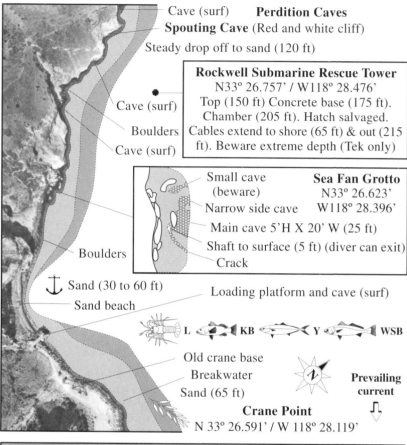

Cave (surf)   **Perdition Caves**
Spouting Cave (Red and white cliff)
Steady drop off to sand (120 ft)

Rockwell Submarine Rescue Tower
N33° 26.757' / W118° 28.476'
Cave (surf)   Top (150 ft) Concrete base (175 ft).
Chamber (205 ft). Hatch salvaged.
Boulders   Cables extend to shore (65 ft) & out (215
Cave (surf)   ft). Beware extreme depth (Tek only)

Small cave   **Sea Fan Grotto**
(beware)   N33° 26.623'
Narrow side cave   W118° 28.396'
Main cave 5'H X 20' W (25 ft)
Shaft to surface (5 ft) (diver can exit)
Boulders   Crack

⚓ Sand (30 to 60 ft)
Sand beach   Loading platform and cave (surf)

L ⟨ KB ⟨ Y ⟨ WSB

Old crane base
Breakwater
Sand (65 ft)   **Prevailing
current**

Crane Point
N 33° 26.591' / W 118° 28.119'

Sea Fan Grotto looking Southwest.

BLUE CAVERN POINT

Lava formations, tunnels and caves. Difficult to anchor
due to depth and preserve. Big Fisherman's Cove home of University of
Southern California / Wrigley Marine Science Center and Catalina Hyperbaric
Chamber. White banks at south of cove are volcanic ash. Private moorings in
cove (possible use in NE storms). Leopard sharks on north side of pier in
summer (snorkel only). Squid in spring. Beware of boat traffic and currents.

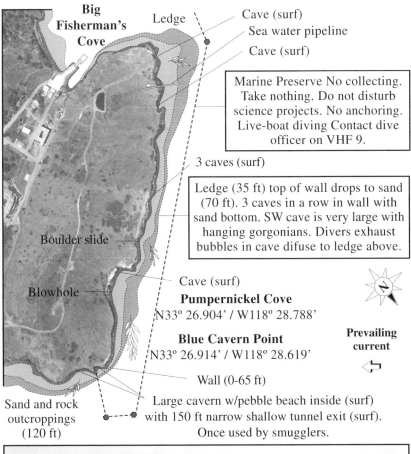

Big Fisherman's Cove

Ledge

Cave (surf)
Sea water pipeline
Cave (surf)

Marine Preserve No collecting.
Take nothing. Do not disturb
science projects. No anchoring.
Live-boat diving Contact dive
officer on VHF 9.

3 caves (surf)

Ledge (35 ft) top of wall drops to sand
(70 ft). 3 caves in a row in wall with
sand bottom. SW cave is very large with
hanging gorgonians. Divers exhaust
bubbles in cave difuse to ledge above.

Boulder slide

Blowhole

Cave (surf)
Pumpernickel Cove
N33° 26.904' / W118° 28.788'

Blue Cavern Point
N33° 26.914' / W118° 28.619'

Prevailing
current

Wall (0-65 ft)

Sand and rock
outcroppings
(120 ft)

Large cavern w/pebble beach inside (surf)
with 150 ft narrow shallow tunnel exit (surf).
Once used by smugglers.

Blue Cavern Point looking Southwest.

HARBOR (ISTHMUS) REEF

Large oblong pinnacle about 500 yds long and
250 yds wide. Pockets of sand, plateaus, ridges and small overhangs.
Sheephead, garibaldi, treefish, senorita, blue-banded goby, senorita,
mackerel, sardine, anchovy, moray eel, horn shark, bat ray (sand), octopus,
coffee bean cowry, Christmas tree worms, gorgonians and harbor seals.
Beware strong currents and boat traffic.

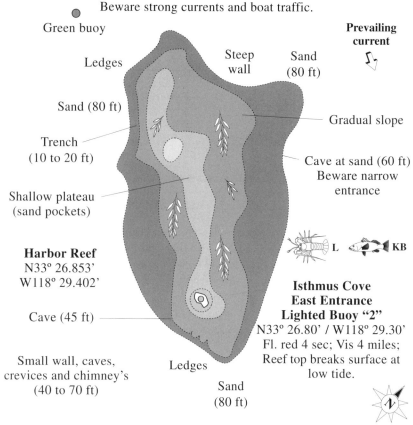

Green buoy

Ledges

Steep wall

Sand (80 ft)

Prevailing current

Sand (80 ft)

Trench (10 to 20 ft)

Gradual slope

Cave at sand (60 ft)
Beware narrow entrance

Shallow plateau (sand pockets)

Harbor Reef
N33° 26.853'
W118° 29.402'

L   KB

**Isthmus Cove
East Entrance
Lighted Buoy "2"**
N33° 26.80' / W118° 29.30'
Fl. red 4 sec; Vis 4 miles;
Reef top breaks surface at
low tide.

Cave (45 ft)

Small wall, caves,
crevices and chimney's
(40 to 70 ft)

Ledges

Sand (80 ft)

Harbor Reef looking Northwest.

BIRD ROCK

Bird Rock (White Rock Island) named for white bird guano covering. Privately owned (not part of the original Catalina land grant). Purchased in July, 1925 for $138 worth of "Valentine Scrip" (created by special land transfer act of Congress). After a legal battle with the Santa Catalina Island Co., title was finally awarded in April 1929. Once proposed as site for gambling casino. Sheephead, garibaldi, blue perch, blacksmith, baitfish, torpedo ray, gorgonians, sea lion and bull kelp. Beware heavy boat traffic, currents and surge.

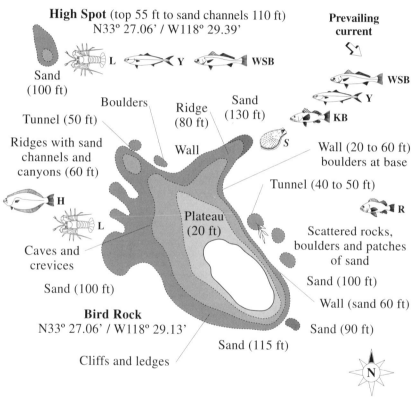

High Spot (top 55 ft to sand channels 110 ft)
N33° 27.06' / W118° 29.39'

Prevailing current

Sand (100 ft)

Boulders

Tunnel (50 ft)

Ridges with sand channels and canyons (60 ft)

Ridge (80 ft)

Wall

Sand (130 ft)

Caves and crevices

Plateau (20 ft)

Wall (20 to 60 ft) boulders at base

Tunnel (40 to 50 ft)

Scattered rocks, boulders and patches of sand

Sand (100 ft)

Sand (100 ft)

Wall (sand 60 ft)

Bird Rock
N33° 27.06' / W118° 29.13'

Sand (90 ft)

Sand (115 ft)

Cliffs and ledges

N

Bird Rock looking Northeast.

TWO HARBORS INFORMATION

General Information: Isthmus Cove and Catalina Harbor form Two Harbors. Private property owned by the Santa Catalina Island Company and administered by Two Harbors Enterprises. Population is about 150. Facilities include a restaurant and bar, snack bar, general store, dive shop, Banning House Lodge (built 1898), camping cabins (Oct - Apr) and nearby campground. Old Civil War barracks (1864) currently used by Isthmus Yacht Club. Only one room schoolhouse (little red) in California. For general information www.scico.com or phone: 310-510-0303.

Mooring: See Mooring Information on page 80.

Anchoring: 300' outside of moorings. See Anchoring Information (pg. 83).

Dinghy Docks: Located at base of the pier. 14' maximum length. Secure using long bow line (painter).

Shoreboat: Services the Isthmus, Fourth and Cherry Coves. Scheduled runs to Emerald and Howlands in the summer. Call for shoreboat on VHF channel 9 or blast horn 3 times for pickup.

Floats: Used for loading and unloading only. Do not leave vessel unattended. Keep a spring line ready during surge.

Generators: Must be turned off from 10 PM to 7 AM.

Alcohol: Private property so open containers are allowed on streets, beach, pier or floats (some restrictions at restaurant and bar).

Trash: All trash is shipped to mainland. Recycling program requires all trash be separated (metal & glass in one bag). Take trash home if possible. Trash boat "Salad Bowl" will pick up on lee side coves in summer (fee charged).

Unattended vessels: Not allowed to leave unattended overnight.

Marine mechanics: Call Harbor Office on VHF channel 09.

Fuel: Available at the pier in winter or fuel dock in summer. Fuel Dock hours are 8 am to 4 pm, year-round. Hours extended in summer.

Water: Available at the pier in winter or fuel dock in summer. Water is in short supply so please conserve (no wash downs). Top off tanks before coming to the Island (thanks).

Propane: Available at the purchasing warehouse.

Showers: Located near administrative offices.

Lodging: Banning House, Camping cabins (Oct - Apr) and camping.

ATM Machine: Located near offices behind bar patio.

Cross Channel Transportation: Catalina Express to San Pedro (310-510-1212) Some trips via Avalon.

Transportation to Avalon: Safari Bus (310-510-2800).

Dogs: Keep on leash at all times. Not allowed on patio or left unattended. Clean up required.

5 Mile per hour or wakeless speed in harbor.

ISTHMUS COVE

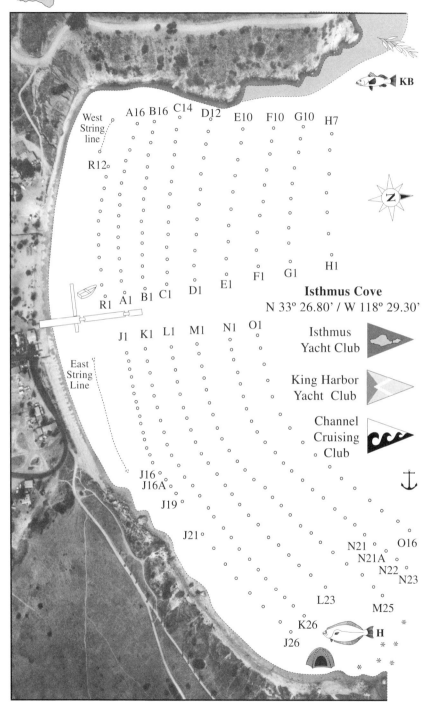

KB

West String line

A16 B16 C14 DJ2 E10 F10 G10 H7

R12

Z

H1

E1 F1 G1

Isthmus Cove
N 33° 26.80' / W 118° 29.30'

R1 A1 B1 C1 D1

J1 K1 L1 M1 N1 O1

Isthmus Yacht Club

East String Line

King Harbor Yacht Club

Channel Cruising Club

J16
J16A

J19

J21

N21
N21A
N22
N23

O16

L23

M25

K26

J26

H

FOURTH OF JULY COVE

Named for 4th of July reunions of the Banning family.
Sheephead. Beware heavy boat traffic. For mooring call Fourth of July
harbormaster on VHF 09.

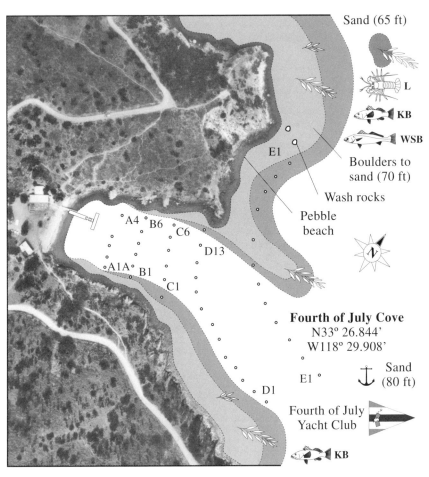

Sand (65 ft)

L

KB

WSB

E1

Boulders to
sand (70 ft)

Wash rocks

Pebble
beach

A4   B6   C6

D13

A1A   B1

C1

Fourth of July Cove
N33° 26.844'
W118° 29.908'

Sand
(80 ft)

E1

Fourth of July
Yacht Club

KB

D1

Fourth of July and Cherry Coves looking Southwest.

CHERRY COVE

Named for grove of cherry trees. Boy Scouts Camp
Cherry Valley (1919). Blue-banded gobi, bat ray and bull kelp. Beware of
boat traffic. For mooring call Cherry Cove harbormaster on VHF 09.

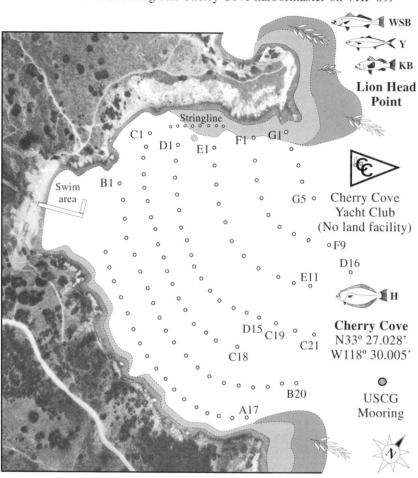

Cherry Cove in 1938.

LION HEAD POINT

Formation resembles head of male lion. Series of
ledges and several caves. Special closed area. Take no invertebrates.
Torpedo ray, sting ray, bat ray and angel sharks. Beware of boat traffic.

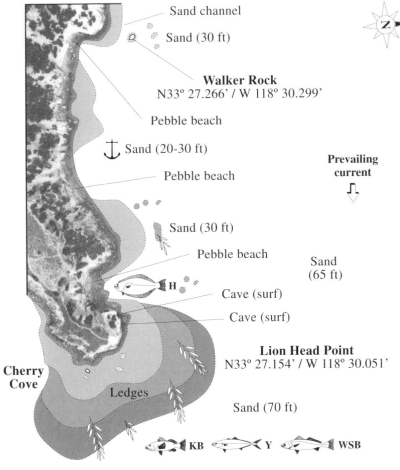

Sand channel

Sand (30 ft)

Walker Rock
N33° 27.266' / W 118° 30.299'

Pebble beach

Sand (20-30 ft)

Pebble beach

**Prevailing
current**

Sand (30 ft)

Pebble beach

Sand
(65 ft)

H

Cave (surf)

Cave (surf)

Lion Head Point
N33° 27.154' / W 118° 30.051'

**Cherry
Cove**

Ledges

Sand (70 ft)

KB   Y   WSB

Lion Head looking Southeast.

SHIP ROCK

Pinnacle (66 ft high), covered with bird guano, named
for appearance similar to a ship's white sail. 1.2 miles from Isthmus.
Plateau has good snorkeling. Sheephead, ling cod, garibaldi, halfmoon,
blacksmith, senorita, kelpfish, blue-banded goby, zebra goby, butterfly fish
(summer), moray eel, mackerel, anchovy, sardine, sharks (horn, swell,
angel), mussel, octopus, squid (spring), nudibranchs (spanish shawl, horned,
phidianas, dendronotus, dorids), sponges, anemone, gorgonians, sea lions
and harbor seals. Beware strong currents, surge and heavy boat traffic.

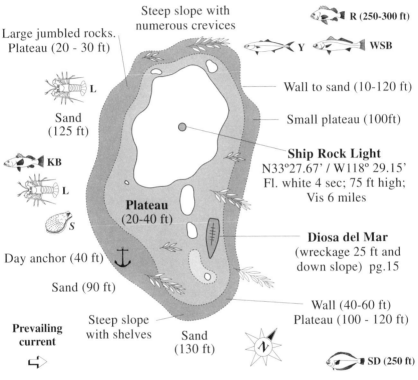

Steep slope with numerous crevices

R (250-300 ft)

Y   WSB

Large jumbled rocks.
Plateau (20 - 30 ft)

Wall to sand (10-120 ft)

L

Small plateau (100ft)

Sand
(125 ft)

Ship Rock Light
N33°27.67' / W118° 29.15'
Fl. white 4 sec; 75 ft high;
Vis 6 miles

KB

L

Plateau
(20-40 ft)

S

Diosa del Mar
(wreckage 25 ft and
down slope) pg.15

Day anchor (40 ft)

Sand (90 ft)

Wall (40-60 ft)
Plateau (100 - 120 ft)

**Prevailing
current**

Steep slope
with shelves

Sand
(130 ft)

SD (250 ft)

Ship Rock looking North.

49

EAGLE REEF

Large reef in three large sections and topped by a series of pinnacles. Small walls, ledges, jumbled rock, small caves, crevices and sand channels. Area about 50 square yards and 1/2 mile (600 yards) offshore. Sheephead, black sea bass, ling cod, sculpin, garibaldi, blacksmith, kelpfish, treefish, senorita, opaleye, blue-banded goby, ghost goby, bat ray, horn shark, swell shark, nudibranchs, anemones (corynactis, zoanthid), gorgonian, sponges, norris top shell, wavy top turban, giant keyhole limpet and elk kelp . Beware of boat traffic and strong currents (use kelp to determine current strength).

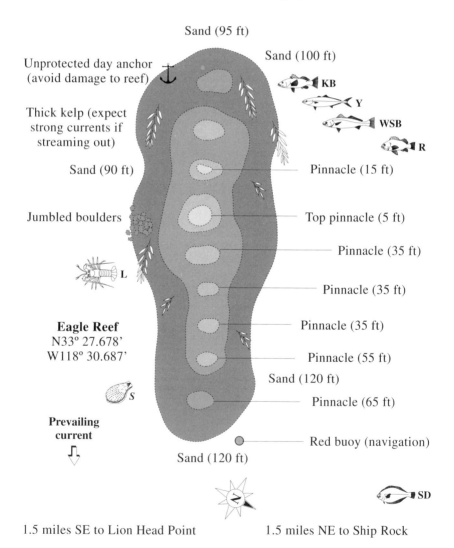

Sand (95 ft)

Sand (100 ft)

Unprotected day anchor (avoid damage to reef)

KB

Y

WSB

R

Thick kelp (expect strong currents if streaming out)

Sand (90 ft)

Pinnacle (15 ft)

Jumbled boulders

Top pinnacle (5 ft)

Pinnacle (35 ft)

L

Pinnacle (35 ft)

Eagle Reef
N33° 27.678'
W118° 30.687'

Pinnacle (35 ft)

Pinnacle (55 ft)

Sand (120 ft)

S

Pinnacle (65 ft)

Prevailing current

Red buoy (navigation)

Sand (120 ft)

SD

1.5 miles SE to Lion Head Point

1.5 miles NE to Ship Rock

50

EEL COVE

Special closed area. Take no invertebrates.

Eel Cove Reef is about 50 yards offshore with a large crack running through reef. Kelp bass, sheephead, garibaldi, blacksmith, kelpfish, blue-banded goby, moray eel, bat rays (sand), lobster (protected), nudibranchs (spanish shawl), sea star, gorgonians, elk kelp and bull kelp. Beware of boat traffic.

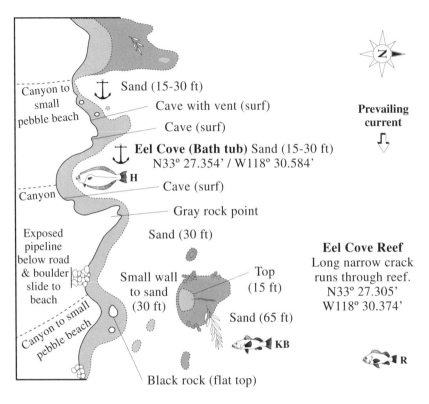

Canyon to small pebble beach

Sand (15-30 ft)

Cave with vent (surf)

Cave (surf)

Eel Cove (Bath tub) Sand (15-30 ft)
N33° 27.354' / W118° 30.584'

H

Cave (surf)

Canyon

Gray rock point

Exposed pipeline below road & boulder slide to beach

Sand (30 ft)

Canyon to small pebble beach

Small wall to sand (30 ft)

Top (15 ft)

Sand (65 ft)

KB

Black rock (flat top)

Prevailing current

Eel Cove Reef
Long narrow crack runs through reef.
N33° 27.305'
W118° 30.374'

R

Flat black rock and Eel Cove looking Southwest.

LITTLE & BIG GEIGER COVES

Special closed area. Take no invertebrates.
Big Geiger (Sullivan's Beach), 1.5 miles W of Isthmus, has good anchorage for 10+ boats. Pipefish (eel grass patch reefs). **Little Geiger** For the only mooring, call Little Geiger Harbormaster on VHF 09. Sheephead, rockfish, garibaldi, blacksmith, senorita, opaleye, leopard shark, bat ray, clams, octopus, lobster (protected), sheep crab and gorgonians.

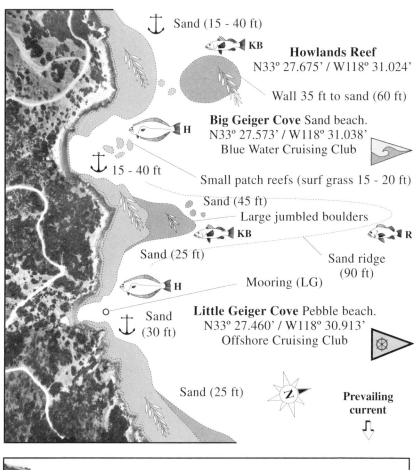

Sand (15 - 40 ft)

KB

Howlands Reef
N33° 27.675' / W118° 31.024'

Wall 35 ft to sand (60 ft)

H

Big Geiger Cove Sand beach.
N33° 27.573' / W118° 31.038'
Blue Water Cruising Club

15 - 40 ft

Small patch reefs (surf grass 15 - 20 ft)

Sand (45 ft)

Large jumbled boulders

KB

R

Sand (25 ft)

Sand ridge
(90 ft)

H

Mooring (LG)

Sand
(30 ft)

Little Geiger Cove Pebble beach.
N33° 27.460' / W118° 30.913'
Offshore Cruising Club

Sand (25 ft)

Z

**Prevailing
current**

Little and Big Geiger Coves looking Southwest.

HOWLAND'S / EMERALD (EAST)

Special closed area. Take no invertebrates.

Howland's has a fresh water well. For mooring call Emerald Bay or Howland's Harbormaster on VHF 09. Sheephead, garibaldi, blacksmith, kelpfish, half moon, opaleye, blue-banded goby, chestnut cowry, norris top snail, nudibranchs, sea stars, gorgonians and elk kelp. Good anchorage.

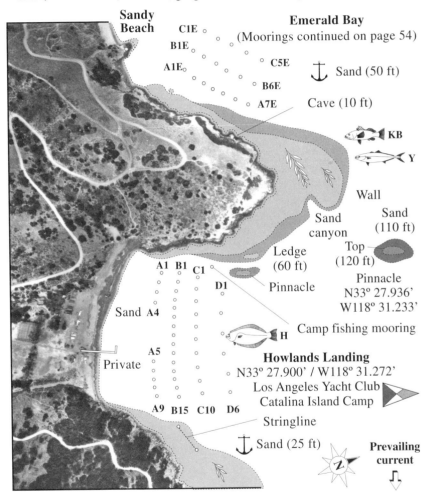

Sandy Beach

C1E
B1E
A1E

Emerald Bay
(Moorings continued on page 54)

C5E

⚓ Sand (50 ft)

B6E

A7E   Cave (10 ft)

KB
Y

Wall

Sand canyon   Sand (110 ft)

Ledge (60 ft)   Top (120 ft)

A1 B1 C1
D1   Pinnacle

Pinnacle
N33° 27.936'
W118° 31.233'

Sand A4

Camp fishing mooring   H

A5

Howlands Landing
N33° 27.900' / W118° 31.272'
Los Angeles Yacht Club
Catalina Island Camp

Private

A9 B15 C10 D6

Stringline

⚓ Sand (25 ft)

Prevailing current

Howlands / Emerald point looking South.

53

EMERALD BAY / INDIAN ROCK

Emerald Bay also called Johnson's Landing.
Boy Scouts of America camp. Special closed area. Take no invertebrates.
Good anchorage. Sheephead, blue-banded goby, bat ray, sheep crab, arrow
crab, nudibranchs and elk kelp.

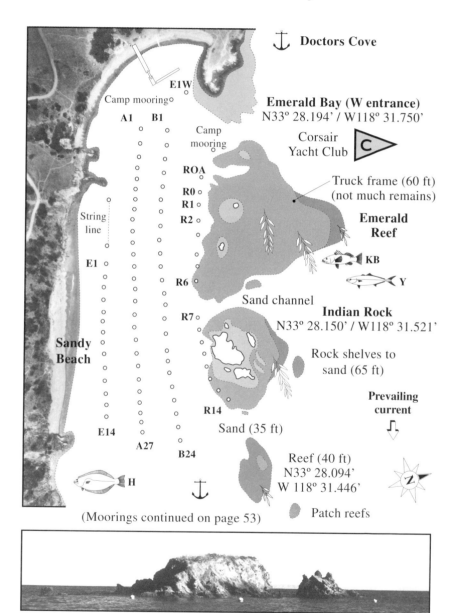

⚓ **Doctors Cove**

E1W

Camp mooring ○

A1   B1

Camp
mooring

Emerald Bay (W entrance)
N33° 28.194' / W118° 31.750'

Corsair
Yacht Club C

ROA

R0
R1
R2

Truck frame (60 ft)
(not much remains)

**Emerald
Reef**

String
line

KB

Y

E1

R6

Sand channel

Indian Rock
N33° 28.150' / W118° 31.521'

R7

Rock shelves to
sand (65 ft)

**Sandy
Beach**

**Prevailing
current**

R14

E14

Sand (35 ft)

A27

B24

Reef (40 ft)
N33° 28.094'
W 118° 31.446'

Z

H   ⚓

Patch reefs

(Moorings continued on page 53)

Indian Rock looking North.

DOCTOR'S COVE

Special closed area. Take no invertebrates.
Good anchorage for 3 to 5 boats. Sheephead, garibaldi, bat ray, torpedo ray, sting ray, horn shark, angel shark, leopard shark, octopus and gorgonians.
Beware of currents and boat traffic.

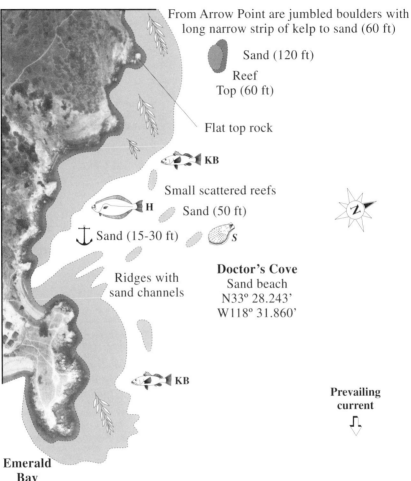

From Arrow Point are jumbled boulders with long narrow strip of kelp to sand (60 ft)

Sand (120 ft)

Reef
Top (60 ft)

Flat top rock

KB

Small scattered reefs

H   Sand (50 ft)

Sand (15-30 ft)   S

Ridges with
sand channels

Doctor's Cove
Sand beach
N33° 28.243'
W118° 31.860'

KB

**Prevailing
current**

**Emerald
Bay**

Doctor's Cove looking Southwest.

ARROW POINT

Sheephead. black sea bass, blacksmith, senorita,
kelpfish, mackerel, anchovies, blue-banded goby, moray eel, nudibranchs
and gorgonians. Beware of surge and currents and boat traffic off point.

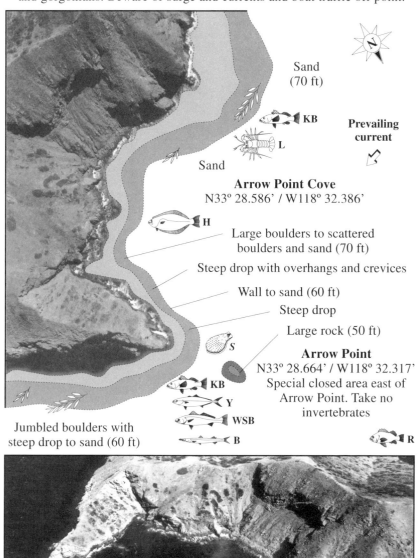

Sand
(70 ft)

KB

L

Prevailing
current

Sand

Arrow Point Cove
N33° 28.586' / W118° 32.386'

H

Large boulders to scattered
boulders and sand (70 ft)

Steep drop with overhangs and crevices

Wall to sand (60 ft)

Steep drop

Large rock (50 ft)

S

Arrow Point
N33° 28.664' / W118° 32.317'
Special closed area east of
Arrow Point. Take no
invertebrates

KB

Y

WSB

Jumbled boulders with
steep drop to sand (60 ft)

B

R

Arrow Point, aerial view, looking East.

PARSON'S LANDING

Parson's Landing formerly called Smuggler's Den.
Spring up canyon. Sheephead, treefish, halfmoon, garibaldi, rockfish,
opaleye, scorpion fish, blue-banded goby, ghost goby, moray eel, leopard
shark, bat ray, gorgonians and elk kelp. Beware of surge, currents and wind.

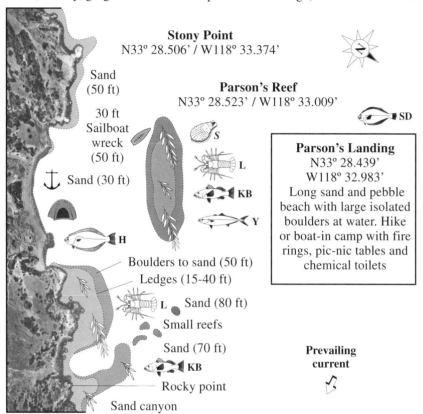

Stony Point
N33° 28.506' / W118° 33.374'

Sand
(50 ft)

Parson's Reef
N33° 28.523' / W118° 33.009'

SD

30 ft
Sailboat
wreck
(50 ft)

S

L

Sand (30 ft)

KB

Y

H

Parson's Landing
N33° 28.439'
W118° 32.983'
Long sand and pebble
beach with large isolated
boulders at water. Hike
or boat-in camp with fire
rings, pic-nic tables and
chemical toilets

Boulders to sand (50 ft)

Ledges (15-40 ft)

L   Sand (80 ft)

Small reefs

Sand (70 ft)

KB

**Prevailing
current**

Rocky point

Sand canyon

Arrow Point and Parson's Landing looking Southeast.

BLACK POINT / JOHNSON'S ROCK

Johnson's Rock protrudes just above surface (beware)
with extensive reef system from rock to shore. Sheephead, garibaldi, bat
ray, angel shark, nudibranchs, sea cucumber, tube anemone, gorgonians and
harbor seals. Eel grass in shallow. **Black Point** (Black Rock) is 1.3 miles
east of West End. Reef extends out with giant boulders which form small
walls, caves and sand channels. Sargo, treefish, horn shark, fragile star,
sheep crab and gorgonians. Beware currents.

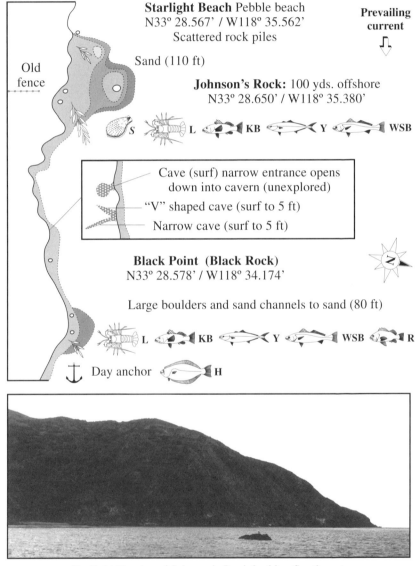

Old fence

Starlight Beach Pebble beach
N33° 28.567' / W118° 35.562'
Scattered rock piles

Sand (110 ft)

Prevailing
current

Johnson's Rock: 100 yds. offshore
N33° 28.650' / W118° 35.380'

S   L   KB   Y   WSB

Cave (surf) narrow entrance opens
down into cavern (unexplored)
"V" shaped cave (surf to 5 ft)
Narrow cave (surf to 5 ft)

Black Point (Black Rock)
N33° 28.578' / W118° 34.174'

Large boulders and sand channels to sand (80 ft)

L   KB   Y   WSB   R

Day anchor   H

Starlight Beach and Johnson's Rock looking Southwest.

WEST END (LAND'S END)

Also called Occidental Point. Gold rumored to be
discovered here in 1830. Most exposed point of the island. Steep walls and
slopes. Steep walls and slopes. Marlin and swordfish (deep water off point).
Mackerel and gorgonians. Keep an eye out for eagles. Beware thermoclines,
heavy surf, surge and currents.

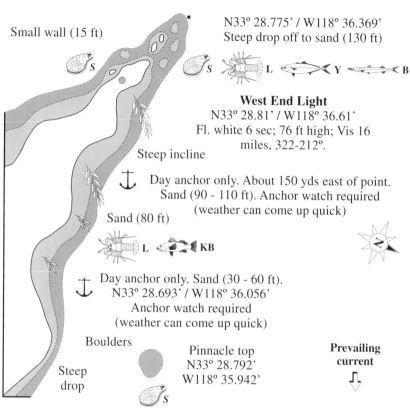

Small wall (15 ft)

N33° 28.775' / W118° 36.369'
Steep drop off to sand (130 ft)

S · L ⟶ Y ⟶ B

West End Light
N33° 28.81' / W118° 36.61'
Fl. white 6 sec; 76 ft high; Vis 16
miles, 322-212°.

Steep incline

⚓ Day anchor only. About 150 yds east of point.
Sand (90 - 110 ft). Anchor watch required
(weather can come up quick)

Sand (80 ft)

L ⟶ KB

⚓ Day anchor only. Sand (30 - 60 ft).
N33° 28.693' / W118° 36.056'
Anchor watch required
(weather can come up quick)

Boulders

Steep
drop

Pinnacle top
N33° 28.792'
W118° 35.942'

**Prevailing
current**
⬇

S

Land's End looking East.

EAGLE ROCK

Named for eagle's nest on top. Also called Finger Rock.
Heavy kelp between Eagle Rock and shore (boaters should not try to run
the gap). Sheephead, ling cod, treefish, sea star, spanish shawl, anemone
and gorgonians. Beware large swell, surge and currents.

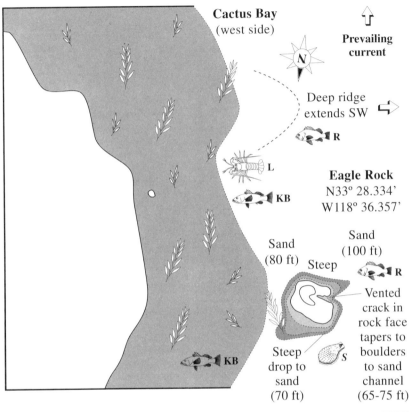

Eagle Rock. Looking Northeast.

CACTUS BAY / STAR BAY

Cactus Bay is 0.9 miles SE of West End.
Sheephead and gorgonians.

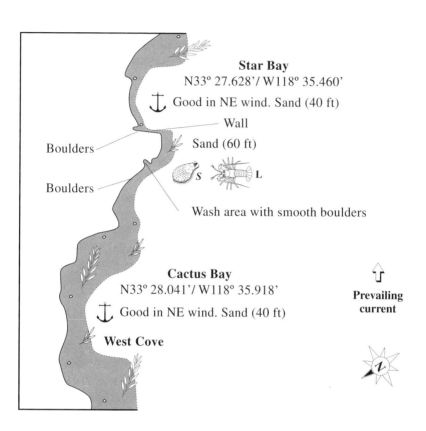

Star Bay
N33° 27.628'/ W118° 35.460'
⚓ Good in NE wind. Sand (40 ft)

— Wall
Sand (60 ft)

S   L

Boulders —

Boulders —

Wash area with smooth boulders

Cactus Bay
N33° 28.041'/ W118° 35.918'
⚓ Good in NE wind. Sand (40 ft)

⇧
**Prevailing
current**

West Cove

Western point of Cactus Bay looking Northeast.

GULL ROCK / IRONBOUND COVE

Surge and currents. Good anchoring in NE wind.
Not good for overnight (too exposed). Sheephead, bat ray and sea lions.
Squid spawn here in the spring.

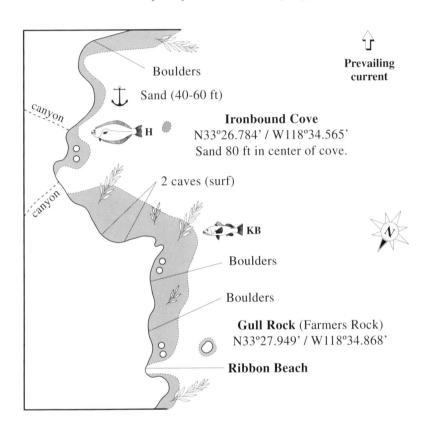

Prevailing
current

Boulders

Sand (40-60 ft)

Ironbound Cove
N33°26.784' / W118°34.565'
Sand 80 ft in center of cove.

canyon

H

2 caves (surf)

canyon

KB

Boulders

Boulders

Gull Rock (Farmers Rock)
N33°27.949' / W118°34.868'

Ribbon Beach

Gull Rock looking East.

RIBBON ROCK

Ribbon Rock is named for light colored quartz ribbons throughout dark rock. Walls, caves and ledges. Holder's "Legends of Torqua" tells of tunnel from Blue Cavern Point to Ribbon Rock used by indian raiders, until sealed at both ends, trapping raiders. Deep anchoring, "live boat" experienced diving or long swim from Ironbound Cove. Sheephead and gorgonians. Beware surge and currents.

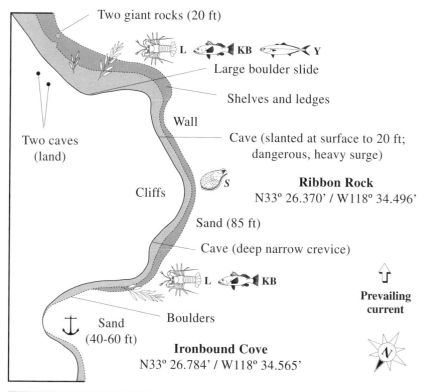

Two giant rocks (20 ft)

L   KB   Y

Large boulder slide

Shelves and ledges

Wall

Two caves (land)

Cave (slanted at surface to 20 ft; dangerous, heavy surge)

Cliffs

S

Ribbon Rock
N33° 26.370' / W118° 34.496'

Sand (85 ft)

Cave (deep narrow crevice)

L   KB

Prevailing current

Sand (40-60 ft)

Boulders

Ironbound Cove
N33° 26.784' / W118° 34.565'

Ribbon Rock looking Northeast.

WHALE ROCK

Whale Rock is named for large wash rock
resembling whales back surfacing. Pinnacles and walls. Sheephead and
gorgonians. Beware currents and surge.

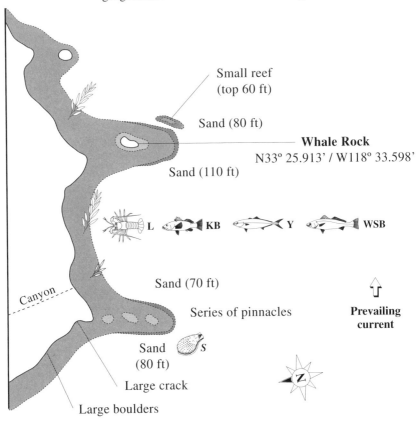

Small reef
(top 60 ft)

Sand (80 ft)

Whale Rock
N33° 25.913' / W118° 33.598'

Sand (110 ft)

L   KB   Y   WSB

Sand (70 ft)

Canyon

Series of pinnacles

**Prevailing
current**

Sand
(80 ft)

S

Large crack

Large boulders

Z

Whale Rock looking Northwest.

KELP POINT

Rocky point. Black sea bass.
Beware surge and currents.

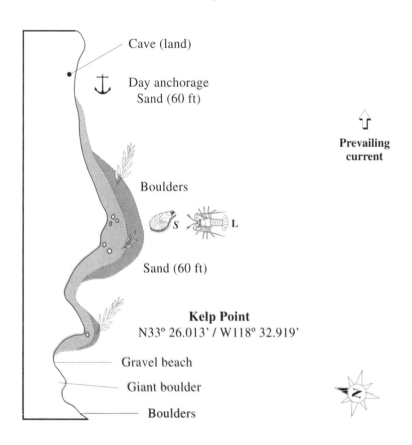

Cave (land)

Day anchorage
Sand (60 ft)

Prevailing
current

Boulders

S L

Sand (60 ft)

Kelp Point
N33° 26.013' / W118° 32.919'

Gravel beach

Giant boulder

Boulders

N

Kelp Point looking Northwest.

CAPE CORTES

Also called "Trident Point" because of three points.
1.2 miles W of Cat Harbor. Pinnacles, canyons and walls. Sheephead, sea
urchin and gorgonians. Beware surge and currents

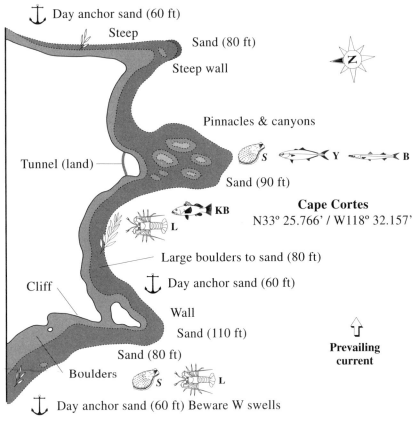

Day anchor sand (60 ft)

Steep

Sand (80 ft)

Steep wall

Pinnacles & canyons

S   Y   B

Tunnel (land)

Sand (90 ft)

KB

L

Cape Cortes
N33° 25.766' / W118° 32.157'

Large boulders to sand (80 ft)

Cliff

Day anchor sand (60 ft)

Wall

Sand (110 ft)

Sand (80 ft)

⇧
**Prevailing
current**

Boulders   S   L

Day anchor sand (60 ft) Beware W swells

Z

Cape Cortes looking Northwest.

LOBSTER BAY

Sheephead and black sea bass (protected).
Beware surge and currents.

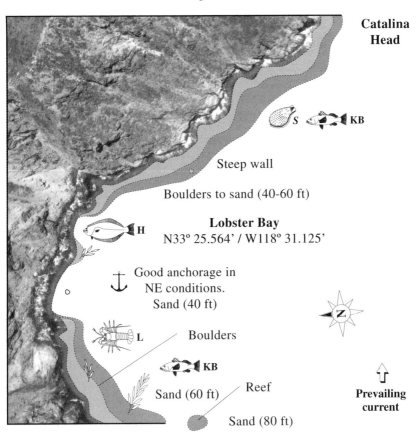

Catalina
Head

S

KB

Steep wall

Boulders to sand (40-60 ft)

Lobster Bay
N33° 25.564' / W118° 31.125'

H

⚓ Good anchorage in
NE conditions.
Sand (40 ft)

Z

L

Boulders

KB

Sand (60 ft)   Reef

⇧
**Prevailing
current**

Sand (80 ft)

Lobster Bay looking North.

CATALINA HEAD

Called Lobster Claw (because of shape). Numerous
caves and crevices. Sheephead, halfmoon, zebra perch and mackerel.
Beware boat traffic, surge, tides and currents.

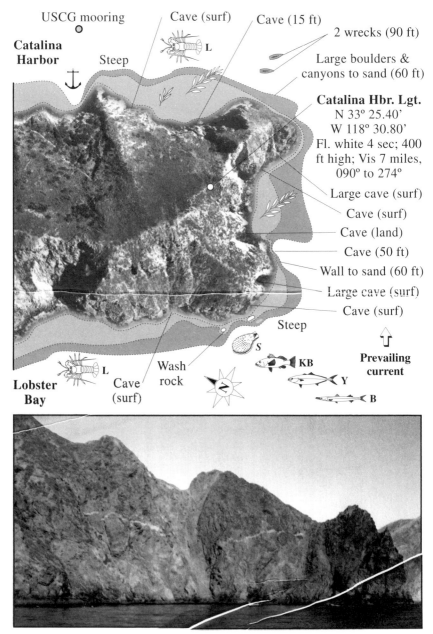

USCG mooring

Catalina Harbor

Steep

Cave (surf)

Cave (15 ft)

2 wrecks (90 ft)

Large boulders &
canyons to sand (60 ft)

Catalina Hbr. Lgt.
N 33° 25.40'
W 118° 30.80'
Fl. white 4 sec; 400
ft high; Vis 7 miles,
090° to 274°

Large cave (surf)

Cave (surf)

Cave (land)

Cave (50 ft)

Wall to sand (60 ft)

Large cave (surf)

Cave (surf)

Steep

Prevailing
current

**Lobster
Bay**

L

Cave
(surf)

Wash
rock

S

KB

Y

B

Catalina Head looking North.

CATALINA HARBOR

N 33° 25.20' / W 118° 30.25'. Calm protected
anchorage (shallow in back harbor). For mooring, call Cat Harbor harbor
patrol on VHF channel 9. Several wrecks (p. 12-14). Many wrecks used in
movies, then abandoned. Poor visibility in back harbor may clear during NE
wind conditions. Beware of heavy boat traffic.

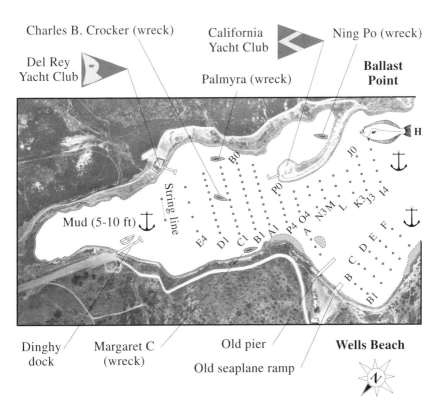

Charles B. Crocker (wreck)

Del Rey
Yacht Club

California
Yacht Club

Palmyra (wreck)

Ning Po (wreck)

**Ballast
Point**

String line

Mud (5-10 ft)

B0

P0

J0

H

E4 D1 C1 B1 A1 P4 O4 A N3 M L K3 J3 I4

B C D E F

B B1

Dinghy
dock

Margaret C
(wreck)

Old pier

Old seaplane ramp

Wells Beach

Early Catalina Harbor showing Ning Po. Ballast Point looking North.

BALLAST POINT / PIN ROCK

Ballast Point was named for the ballast rock
dropped by the early clipper ships to paint hull bottom. Fort Tripoli film set
built in 1926 for film "Old Ironsides."

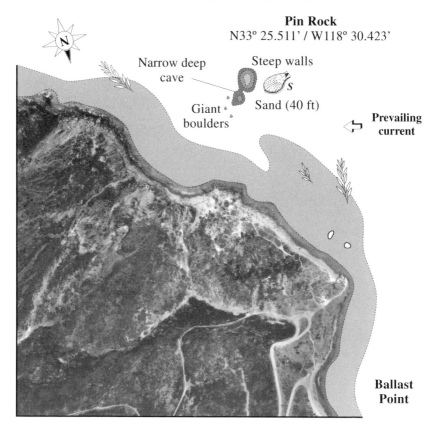

Pin Rock
N33° 25.511' / W118° 30.423'

Narrow deep cave

Steep walls

Sand (40 ft)

Giant boulders

Prevailing current

Ballast Point

Pin Rock. Looking Northwest.

PEDESTAL ROCK

Pinnacle about 200 yards off **Landslide Point**.
Boulder slide off point continues into water. Sand bass, horn sharks and
gorgonians. Beware surge at point.

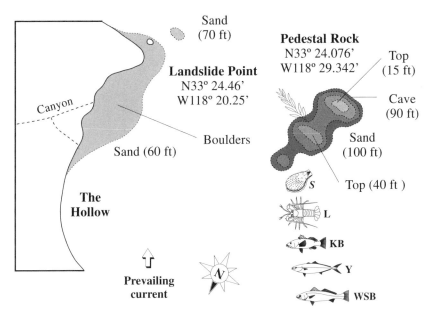

Pedestal Rock (at buoy) looking East toward Landslide Point.

FRED ROCK

Discovered while diving with Fred.
Pinnacle (split top, fissures and canyons) about 150 yards off small beach.
Series of patchy reefs off point.

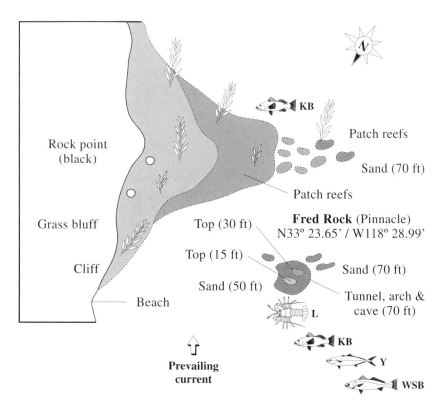

Rock point (black)

Grass bluff

Cliff

Beach

KB

Patch reefs

Sand (70 ft)

Patch reefs

Fred Rock (Pinnacle)
N33° 23.65' / W118° 28.99'

Top (30 ft)

Top (15 ft)

Sand (50 ft)

Sand (70 ft)

Tunnel, arch &
cave (70 ft)

L

KB

Y

WSB

**Prevailing
current**

Rock point (black) looking East.

LITTLE HARBOR

Little Harbor was once site of a large Native Islander settlement. Little Harbor hotel (1894). "Guadalcanal Diary" filmed here. Boat-in or hike-in campground. Reef offers protection for bow and stern anchoring. Beach diving, snorkeling and hiking. Surfing at **Shark Harbor**. Sheephead, black sea bass, mackerel.

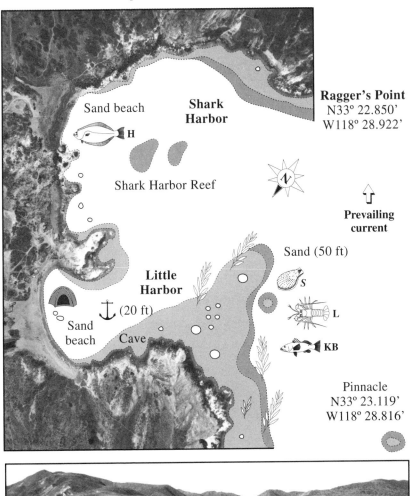

Sand beach

Shark Harbor

H

Ragger's Point
N33° 22.850'
W118° 28.922'

N

Shark Harbor Reef

⇧
Prevailing current

Sand (50 ft)

Little Harbor

⚓ (20 ft)

S

L

Sand beach   Cave

KB

Pinnacle
N33° 23.119'
W118° 28.816'

Little Harbor looking from top of Ragger's Point.

SENTINEL ROCKS / BEN WESTON

Ben Weston is 3.6 miles SE of Catalina Harbor.
also called Mills Landing or Craigs Beach. Best surfing on the Island. Ben
Weston house (1885). **Ben Weston Beach** Exposed rocky points. Black sea
bass, sheephead, blue perch and squid (spring). Beware of surge and poor
visibility.

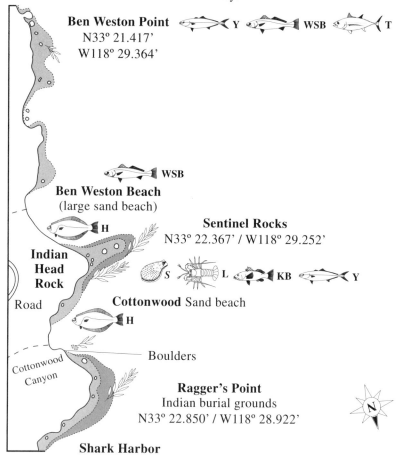

Ben Weston Point — Y — WSB — T
N33° 21.417'
W118° 29.364'

WSB

Ben Weston Beach
(large sand beach)

H

Sentinel Rocks
N33° 22.367' / W118° 29.252'

**Indian
Head
Rock**

Road

S — L — KB — Y

Cottonwood Sand beach

H

Boulders

Cottonwood
Canyon

Ragger's Point
Indian burial grounds
N33° 22.850' / W118° 28.922'

N

Shark Harbor

Sentinel Rocks looking East.

FARNSWORTH BANK

N33° 20.619' W118° 30.994'

Course 55° (1.8 miles) to Ben Weston Point and 319° to Catalina Harbor. This series of seamounts surrounded by open ocean. Named for, Catalina sportfishing legend, George Farnsworth. One of the best diving and fishing spots Catalina has to offer. Pinnacles, spires, plateaus (with sinkholes), ledges, sheer walls, caves and canyons. Covering and area over 1/2 mile from E to W. **Marine preserve (no corals, marine plants or geological specimans may be taken).** Covered by California hydrocoral (not a true coral). Color ranges frome purple to pink. Largest (over 24" clusters) found over 100 ft. Coral grows very slowly and perpendicular to current. Small purple slipper snail (parasitie) often found on branches. Avoid damage to reef when anchoring. Black seabass, sculpin, ling cod, sheephead, ocean whitefish, blue rockfish (few places found on the island), garibaldi, treefish, blacksmith, senorita, gobies, bonito, mackerel, sardine, moray eel, blue shark, torpedo ray, shrimp, crabs, sea star, nudibranchs, anemones (strawberry and solitary), sponges, gorgonians and sea lions. Very exposed so good conditions are a must. Beware of weather changes, surf, surge, and currents. Divers pay attention to buoyancy, air consumption and depth.

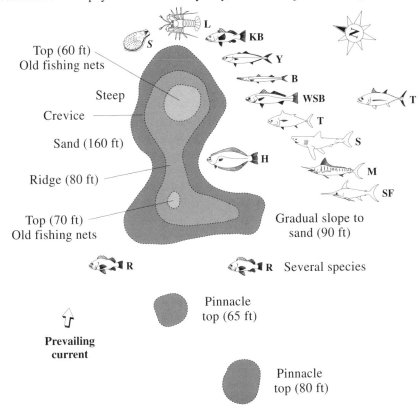

Top (60 ft)
Old fishing nets

Steep

Crevice

Sand (160 ft)

Ridge (80 ft)

Top (70 ft)
Old fishing nets

Gradual slope to
sand (90 ft)

Several species

Prevailing
current

Pinnacle
top (65 ft)

Pinnacle
top (80 ft)

75

CHINA POINT

Named for camp used to smuggle illegal Chinese immigrants (government banned chinese immigration in mid 19th century). Numerous rocky points. Reefs of small to very large boulders with patches of sand. Black sea bass (protected), sheephead, guitarfish, squid, gray moon sponge, sea lions and seals. Outer, open waters may have mola mola, blue shark, jellyfish and an occasional sea turtle passing by the point. Keep an eye out for eagles. Island may block VHF radio. Beware heavy surf, surge, currents and poor visibility.

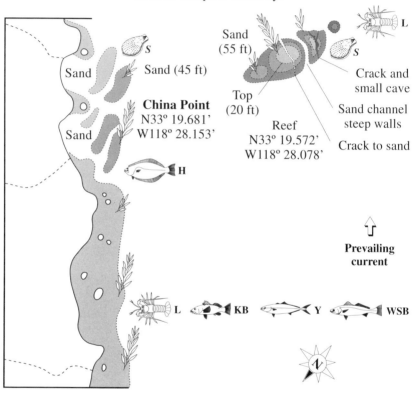

Sand

Sand (45 ft)

China Point
N33° 19.681'
W118° 28.153'

Sand

Sand
(55 ft)

Top
(20 ft)

Reef
N33° 19.572'
W118° 28.078'

Crack and
small cave

Sand channel
steep walls

Crack to sand

Prevailing
current

L   KB   Y   WSB

China Point looking East.

SALTA VERDE POINT

Salta Verde has shallow reefs and scattered rock piles.
Silver Canyon has good anchorage in calm weather or NE wind. Fresh
water flows (part time). Sand bass, sheephead, black sea bass (protected)
and squid (spring). Island may block VHF radio. Beware of surge and poor
visibility

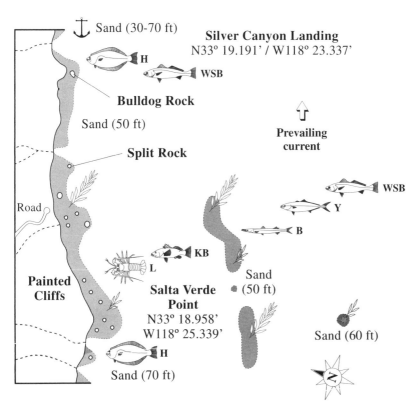

Sand (30-70 ft)

Silver Canyon Landing
N33° 19.191' / W118° 23.337'

H

WSB

Bulldog Rock

Sand (50 ft)

Split Rock

↑
**Prevailing
current**

Road

WSB

Y

B

KB

L

**Painted
Cliffs**

**Salta Verde
Point**
N33° 18.958'
W118° 25.339'

Sand
(50 ft)

Sand (60 ft)

H

N

Sand (70 ft)

Salta Verde Point looking West.

PALISADES & THE V'S

Palisades are sandstone cliffs. Primary squid spawning area. Numerous commercial squid boats in Spring. **The V's are** Three deep canyons. Beautiful waterfalls in heavy rain. Black sea bass and harbor seals. Beware surge and usually poor visibility.

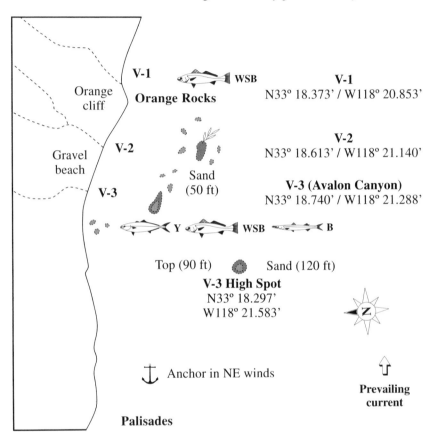

V-1
Orange cliff
Orange Rocks WSB

V-2
Gravel beach

V-3
Sand (50 ft)

Y WSB B

Top (90 ft) Sand (120 ft)

V-3 High Spot
N33° 18.297'
W118° 21.583'

Anchor in NE winds

Palisades

V-1
N33° 18.373' / W118° 20.853'

V-2
N33° 18.613' / W118° 21.140'

V-3 (Avalon Canyon)
N33° 18.740' / W118° 21.288'

Prevailing current

The V's looking North.

CHURCH ROCK

Also called Cathedral Rock. 38' high. Named for
verticle rock faces resembling church steeple. Caves, rock piles and walls.
Middle of reef is a small alcove of boulders with tunnels and caves.
Seaward side is thick feather boa kelp. Exposed to south and west swells.
East side is more protected from prevailing current for day anchor. An area
where currents mix. Sheephead, black sea bass, schools of baitfish,
blacksmith, garibaldi, senorita, angel shark, moray eel, torpedo ray, bat ray,
squid (Spring), nudibranchs, anemone, gorgonians and sponges. Beware of
surge, currents, boat traffic and poor visibility. Island may block VHF.

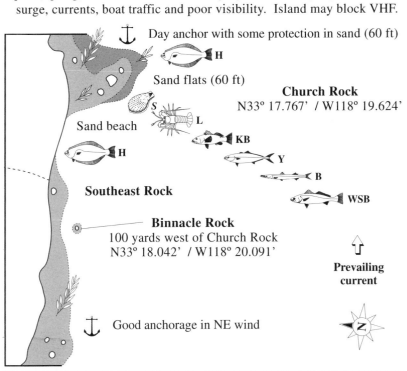

Day anchor with some protection in sand (60 ft)

H

Sand flats (60 ft)

Church Rock
N33° 17.767' / W118° 19.624'

S

L

Sand beach

H

KB

Y

B

Southeast Rock

WSB

Binnacle Rock
100 yards west of Church Rock
N33° 18.042' / W118° 20.091'

**Prevailing
current**

Good anchorage in NE wind

Church Rock looking Northeast.

OFFSHORE BANKS

Most banks are named for the number of fathoms listed on the chart showing the top of the bank. Deep water (offshore) fishing for pelagics (blue water fish) is most productive over sub-sea mountain ranges (banks). In these areas, upwellings bring rich, nutrient laden water to the surface feeding algae blooms and attracting microscopic animals (plankton). Huge schools of small bait fish come to feed, which attracts marlin, swordfish, tuna, sharks and other predators. **Avalon Bank (228):** 6.2 M 039° Avalon Harbor. **Southeast (SE) End:** 3 M off Church Rock.

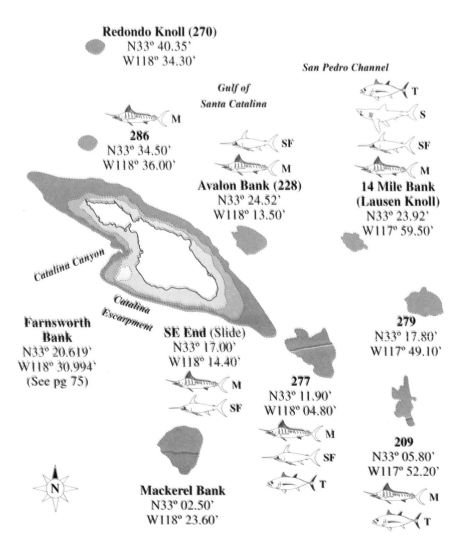

Redondo Knoll (270)
N33° 40.35'
W118° 34.30'

San Pedro Channel

*Gulf of
Santa Catalina*

T

S

M

SF

286
N33° 34.50'
W118° 36.00'

SF

M

Avalon Bank (228)
N33° 24.52'
W118° 13.50'

SF

M

**14 Mile Bank
(Lausen Knoll)**
N33° 23.92'
W117° 59.50'

Catalina Canyon

*Catalina
Escarpment*

279
N33° 17.80'
W117° 49.10'

**Farnsworth
Bank**
N33° 20.619'
W118° 30.994'
(See pg 75)

SE End (Slide)
N33° 17.00'
W118° 14.40'

M

SF

277
N33° 11.90'
W118° 04.80'

M

SF

T

209
N33° 05.80'
W117° 52.20'

M

T

N

Mackerel Bank
N33° 02.50'
W118° 23.60'

III. BOATING INFORMATION

Information on magnetic courses, anchoring, mooring and wrap ups.

Boating Basics

- Be a responsible boat operator
- Learn and practice good boating skills
- Use proper VHF radio etiquette
- Plan your trip and check the weather
  (Beware Santana, NE, winds from Nov-Mar)
- Prepare emergency procedures and equipment

MAGNETIC COURSE & NAUTICAL MILES

For reference only (not for use in navigation)

	West End N33°29.00' W118°37.00'	Isthmus N33°57.5'? W118°28.00'	Long Pt. N33°57.5'? W118°28.00'	Avalon N33°20.83' W118°19.33'	East End N33°17.80' W118°18.60'
Marina Del Rey (South entrance) N33°57.50' W118°27.80'	181/001 30 NM	163/348 30 NM			
Redondo Beach (Bell buoy #1) N33°50.30' W118°23.80'	194/014 24 NM				
Los Angeles/San Pedro (LA - approach buoy) N33°42.00' W118°14.50'	221/041 23 NM	204/024 20 NM	184/004 19 NM	177/357 22NM	172/352 24 NM
Long Beach (LB - approach buoy) N33°42.10' W118°11.00'	222/042 26 NM	209/029 22 NM	192/012 21 NM	183/003 23 NM	179/359 25 NM
Newport Beach (Bell buoy #1) N33°35.10' W117°52.60'	247/067 37 NM	241/061 32 NM	232/052 27 NM	224/044 26.7 NM	218/038 27.8 NM
Dana Point (1/2 M off) N33°26.80' W117°41.50'	258/078 45 NM	256/076 39 NM	251/071 34 NM	246/066 33 NM	241/061 32.5 NM
Oceanside (Harbor entrance) N33°10.73' W117°24.00'		271/091 58 NM	270/090 51 NM	268/088 47 NM	264/084 45.8 NM
Point Loma N32°39.80' W117°14.50'			296/116 71 NM	294/114 68 NM	292/112 66 NM

1 nautical mile (6076 ft) = 1 mile (5280 ft)

ANCHORING

For many, anchoring is an ordeal, only attempted when moorings are unavailable. Anchoring at Catalina is free and gives you access to areas with no moorings. Little Harbor, Catalina Harbor, Doctors, Little and Big Geiger, Little Fisherman, Cabrillo (Gibraltar), Whites, Willow and numerous small coves have excellent anchorage. With this freedom comes responsibility and courtesy. You must anchor properly for the situation and provide an adequate anchor system for your vessel. Practice anchoring.

Anchor gear will vary. Danforth, CQR (plow) and Bruce anchors are common. For rode, use chain or a combination or nylon line and chain, secured to the anchor with a shackle (seized). Secure the bitter end to prevent loss. On my 40 foot sailboat, I have a 35 lb. CQR with 350 feet of 5/8" chain, a windlass and dual bow rollers on the bow. On the stern is a 20 lb. Hi-tensile Danforth with 60 ft. of chain and 300 ft of nylon line. Stow gear in a vented locker. Your local marine store can suggest gear for your particular vessel. Mark your line (plastic) or chain with (paint).

Pick a good sheltered anchorage with a sand or mud bottom. Survey the conditions including weather and adequate depth. Have the anchor ready to run out (should always be ready). Plan your approach. Observe other boats in the anchorage. In deep water, when using a single anchor, allow room for boats to swing. Don't anchor too deep (not enough scope). In shallow water, bow and stern anchors may be used to prevent swing and allow more boats to anchor. Smaller vessels can anchor closer to shore.

Approach into the wind, drop the anchor and lay out the rode while backing down. The amount to lay out is determined by depth and conditions. Generally the scope (length of rode divided by depth of water) is at least 7 to 1. Cleat off the anchor and back down to set the anchor. When using a stern anchor, let out more rode on the bow, back down toward shore, drop the stern anchor and pull forward. The stern anchor may be placed closer to shore by using a dinghy. Secure all lines and note position. Check periodically (anchor watch) to insure anchor is secure. Change in weather, tide, kelp on the bottom or a poor set can cause the anchor to drag. If dragging, reset the anchor and possibly increase scope. Always use an anchor light at night.

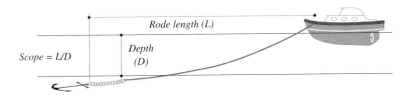

Rode length (L)

Depth (D)

Scope = L/D

MOORING INFORMATION

Most moorings at Catalina are privately owned or leased. Owners have priority to reserve the mooring or assign it to another boat. Remaining moorings are available on a first-come, first-serve basis. Mooring assignments are not guaranteed, you may have to relocate. Fees are usually paid upon arrival and must be paid before departure. Contact the harbor patrol to extend your stay. Moorings can fill up in the summer. Rafting boats together is a possibility so bring fenders. Always be ready to anchor.

Moorings in Avalon Harbor, Descanso and Hamilton Coves are administered by the City of Avalon Harbor Department. The main office is on the end of the main pier. They monitor VHF channels 16 and 12 (working channel), but no mooring assignments are done on the radio. To get a mooring, bring your boat to the main harbor entrance and see the red and gray harbor patrol boat for assignment. Have documentation or CF number and boat length information ready. Fees are based on length of vessel (cash or check). Check out is 9 AM.

Moorings in Two Harbors (Isthmus), Moonstone Cove, White's Landing, Buttonshell, Fourth of July Cove, Cherry Cove, Little Geiger, Howland's Landing, Emerald Bay, Wells Beach and Catalina Harbor are leased from the State of California and administered by the Two Harbors Harbor Department. The main office is on the pier at Two Harbors. They monitor VHF channel 09. To get a mooring, bring your boat to the desired cove and contact the harbor patrol of that cove by VHF for instructions. Fees are based on the size of the mooring (cash, check or credit card at office). Check out is 8 am.

After assignment and prior to approaching the mooring, both Captain and crew should have a plan. Keep a boat hook ready as the mooring wand may lay flat in the water. Know and use the wind and currents (observe how other boats and mooring poles sit). Occasionally the mooring line may be fouled around the mooring can or with kelp. Call the harbor patrol, chances are you will need help. Slowly pull the boat up to the mooring and stop the boat. Grab the pickup pole and pull up to the large yellow loop (bow hawser located about 6' below the surface) and place the on the bow cleat or bit. Be smooth and efficient as the boat will not stay still for long. Put the pole on deck (prevents bumping). Attached to the loop is the smaller spreader (sand) line. Pull the line up and walk it back to the stern of the boat. Watch out for barnacles, fishhooks and broken fiberglass wands (gloves may help). Don't pull the spreader under the boat or it may hang up on keel, rudder, stabilizer or worse, the prop (see wrap up on pg. 86). At the stern, pull up the stern hawser loop and place on the stern cleat. Moorings are set to a specific size. If you can't reach the stern hawser loop, pull up snug and tie off the spreader line to the cleat. Propper line tension is important. Tying off too tight may be hard to release or drag the mooring weight and too loose may drift closer to your neighbor. A dock line, run through the stern hawser eye and back to the stern cleat can help to release or adjust the mooring. Extreme tides may require periodic adjustment to the stern line (take up or let out slack). Recheck bow and stern connections to make sure you're secure. Drop the slack spreader into the water. Sailboats tend to drift past the mooring (headway) so make sure to stop the boat at the pole. Power boats tend to throttle back, often pulling the pole away from the bow crew. Some have stabilizers which may hang up the spreader. Many don't have deck space along the side and should be prepared to pass the spreader to the stern (unbutton canvas, use pipe poles or special sliders). If too close to another boat, try switching lines to that side.

Winter mooring brings some changes. Special winter rates go into effect. Pay for two days and get the next five consecutive days free. Avalon winter rates begin Oct. 15th. Avalon also has a special (shoulder) weekly rate one month between summer and winter rates (pay Thur. through Sun. and get Mon. through Wed. free). Two Harbors winter rates begin Nov. 1st and add a $2 weekly surcharge. Avalon maintains 24 hour harbor patrol service year round (same procedures). Special winter mooring procedures go into effect on moorings administered by the Two Harbors Harbor Department. If unable to contact the harbor patrol by VHF (especially in outer coves), pick up any available mooring. Stay off the first few rows and allow an extra mooring space between boats for safety. The patrol boat will come by in the morning to collect mooring fees. On Isthmus moorings only (due to possible Santa Ana winds from the northeast) all boats are moored facing out to seaward. This means picking up the mooring backward. In this situation the mooring can will be at the stern. Make sure to get the large hawser loop on the bow of the boat. If the mooring is too large, tie off the spreader line on the stern. Try to leave an empty mooring between boats for safety during the winter.

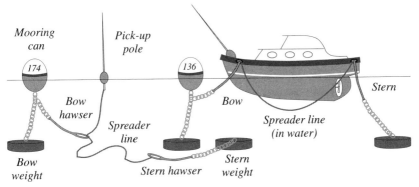

When leaving the mooring, check that the spreader line is not fouled. Drop the stern line into the water making sure the hawser and spreader have time to sink below the hull and prop(s). This is important to prevent fouling the prop, the dreaded wrap up (pg. 86). Release the bow hawser and toss the pole overboard. Be aware of the pole and mooring (don't run over them).

85

WRAP UP (fouled prop)

"Wrap up" is the bad thing that can occur when picking up or leaving a mooring. The propeller(s) become entangled in the wand line, spreader, hawser or worst of all, the chain. Causes include running over the pick up pole, kelp on the spreader (holding the line up or dragging it into prop), currents flaring the spreader out, dinghy tow lines, dangling dock or sheet lines and backing the engine down while pulling the line into the prop(s). This often results in the engine stalling out.

Don't panic! Call the harbor patrol and advise them of your situation. They can help re-secure your vessel. You may be able to use a boat hook to grab the spreader line from behind the prop and pull the line up and secure it to a cleat. Don't restart the engine and try to power out. This will fail 99 percent of the time and may cause serious damage to your vessel and the mooring. A line wrapped on a prop and shaft while the engine is revved up and jammed into gear (Archimedes screw effect) can pull the chain up to the prop (bad), pull the shaft out (very bad) or pull the engine off its mounts (extremely bad).

You need a diver! The harbor patrol will assist in contacting the diving service. A professional service will keep damages lower than using a novice diver. Remember, you are responsible for divers fees and any damages to the mooring gear. In Avalon, the patrol officer will fill out a green card with billing information and description of any mooring damage. You must provide a drivers license and sign the card. A bill will be mailed for any mooring damages. They will give you information on contacting one of several diving services. Divers fees are paid at time of service. In Two Harbors, the harbor patrol will contact the diving service for you and both mooring damage and diving fees are payable when service is rendered..

If you decide to dive it yourself, here are a few tips. Reconsider! I give the average boater about a ten percent chance of success (very generous) and a diver about sixty percent. Both will tend to do excessive damage to the mooring equipment. If you must, here we go! Get slack on both ends of the line leading from the prop (tie off a dock line to the mooring line to relieve tension). Look over the situation, find the key wrap and try to unlock it. If not too tight, turning the prop (by hand) may help loosen the wrap. Avoid using the knife as it may create a mess and will damage the mooring. If you must, cut only the key wrap. When loose, make sure the spreader is clear of the boat. If cut, tie the spreader line back together (severed line will sink to the bottom and diver retrieval fee will be charged). Inspect the prop, struts and hull for damage (a pro knows best what to look for). Go into the engine room and check engine mounts, shaft and shaft log. Remember, you are responsible for mooring damage.

IV. DIVING INFORMATION

Information on diving safety snd emergencies.
Special articles on kelp, kayak and shark diving.

Annual
Gold Star Dive

2nd weekend in July

**Proceeds to benefit the Los Angeles County Sheriff's Department
Avalon S.T.A.R. Program (Success Through Awareness and Resistance)
and the Catalina Hyperbaric Chamber.**

SAFE DIVING PRACTICES

1. Get in shape.
Diving can be physically and mentally exhausting. Be prepared.

2. Maintain good diving skills.
Continuing education and practice.

3. Use well maintained equipment.
Including a submersible pressure gauge, buoyancy compensator with inflator and alternate air source. Inspect gear prior to diving.

4. Avoid using drugs and alcohol.

5. Plan the dive.
Review emergency procedures, buddy system, dive sites and conditions. Observe all local laws including dive flags, Fish and Game regulations.

6. No decompression dives.
Most everything is 60 feet deep or less. Know how to use the dive tables. Ascend at proper rate. Plan and use safety stops.

7. Practice good bouyancy controls.
Adjust weight belt for easy release. Don't overweight. Use relaxed breathing (never hold your breath). Avoid skip breathing and hyperventilation.

8. Dive within personal ability.
Avoid overexertion.

9. Use surface support.
If possible use a float or boat.

10. Use good judgement.
Common sense, knowledge and training will help to avoid panic.

EMERGENCY DIVING PROCEDURES

Several agencies provide guidelines in emergency situations. Divers Alert Network (DAN) is considered the leader. The procedures listed below are a simple one page outline adapted for Catalina Island. Review emergency plans prior to diving.

---

1. Floatation (Get to the surface).
Inflate the buoyancy compensator and drop the weight belt.

2. Call for help.
Signal or yell for help. If possible, have someone contact Baywatch.

3. Get to the boat or to shore.
Aiding a victim in the water is difficult.

4. Maintain airway, breathing and circulation.
Lay the victim on his back. An unconscious victim may require CPR or First Aid. If nauseated, roll onto either side. Treat for shock. If embolism is suspected, elevate the legs a few inches.

5. Contact emergency services.
Contact (VHF radio) Baywatch or U.S. Coast Guard or Harbor Patrol or call 911. Remember to state that it is a "diving emergency." Give the location and type of vessel.

6. Administer oxygen.
If available.

7. Get medical attention.
Follow directions of emergency agencies or transport to nearest medical facility.

8. Keep vital information
Note dive history, time and personal information. Keep all equipment together.

FREE DIVING / HUNTING

Free diving equipment must be comfortable and streamlined. Most SCUBA gear will double for use in free diving. A low volume, good fitting, mask uses less air to clear. Type of fins are determined by an individual's strength and ability. Longer fins generate more power using a slower kick. Large bore snorkel for easy breathing. Wet suit (black, blue or cammo) is snug fitting and comfortable. Use a well balanced weight belt with quick release set opposite of the gun hand. Wear at least one glove for fish handling. Carry a quality, small, sharp knife to cut tangled line. The spear gun should be long and powerful for penetration and accuracy. Most pros prefer rubber band powered guns (reliable) with wood stocks (metal tends to amplify noise). A 48 inch gun is a good basic gun for the Island with a shorter gun for shallow and sand. Long (50-60 in) blue water guns (3/8 in shaft), as powerful as you can load, are used for open water. Trailing surface floats (75 ft line) and reels (150 feet line) are attached to the gun to help fight fish or release gun. Use double barbed detachable tips for open water and keep them sharp. Be safe, cover the tip (cork or rubber) when not in use. Never cock the gun out of the water. If possible, have a buddy hand the gun in and out of the boat. Keep gear well maintained.

Free diving skills must be practiced and developed before hunting becomes efficient. Get in shape! Good physical condition, especially cardiovascular and legs are important. First make a few short dives to purge the wetsuit of excess air. Take a maximum of 2 to 3 deep breaths (avoid hyperventilation). Plan the breath for the entire dive. Leave enough air in reserve for the trip back to the surface. Be comfortable, keeping mind and body relaxed. Avoid gasping for air at the surface. Rest a few minutes between dives. Find a good working depth and set the weight belt to neutral at that depth. The objective is not to dive deep but to get fish. Leg cramps may occur from fatigue or fins that are too large. If this happens rest on the surface and use fingers to massage the cramp or try holding the tip of the fin and straighten the leg. If cramps persist, call it quits for the day. Get aquainted and comfortable with your gun. Learn its range, power and balance. Speargun accuracy should be practiced before diving. The spear shaft must be straight and must be checked. Try shooting at kelp leaves or a suspended plastic bottle. Learn the characteristics of bait fish and try to hang with them. Do they accept you (good) or take off when you approach (more practice).

When stalking, move slowly and silently (stealth mode) using a smooth flutter kick. Drift or glide when possible. While surface scouting, breathe quietly and slowly move head from side to side. The slightest movement or noise will alert the fish, causing it to instantly disappear. Try to be invisible through minimal movement, concealment and silence. Use any available cover (kelp, reef, etc.) especially on descent. Hide in school of bait fish. Bait fish movement can be a good indicator of predators. Submerge using a smooth pike dive without using the arms. Remove the snorkel during descent to avoid bubbles and replace on ascent. Clear the snorkel using the head roll technique to avoid a noisy blast. This is hunting, and the blue water, reefs, kelp and sand are your realm. Learn the ocean environment. Weather, visiblity, currents, tides, surge, temperature and thermoclines are constantly changing. Focus your attention, maximize your peripheral vision and try to sense and feel everything around you. Try not to look directly at the fish (they seem to sense it). Listen, it's quiet underwater but not silent. Learn to recognize small subtle movements, color changes, the camoflaged and hidden. Learn your prey. Gamefish are hard to find and approach. Observe fish reactions and habits in different situations. A colony defense system enables a single fish to quickly warn all others. Focus on fish or other specific objects to maintain reference. Fish have a great sense of smell, so avoid colognes, oils, deodorant, urinating in your wetsuit etc... Experience and learning from mistakes provides the best way to develop hunting techniques and overcome fears.

Be ready to shoot, keeping the gun steady at eye level with arm fully

extended. A straight arm will aid in accuracy and help absorb the shock (kick) of the gun. There's very little time to prepare a shot and any movement will alert the fish. Aim at a spot just behind the gill plate at the center of the spine. Fish are a moving target so you must lead the fish. Fish speed, distance and characteristics of your gun will determine how much. Squeeze the trigger as soon as the fish is lined up. Take only a good clear shot. A wounded fish can't be followed and will be lost.

Once shot, go after the fish and prepare for a fight. Reach through the gills and out the mouth (not sheephead) or put thumb and finger in eye sockets for a good grip. Hold tight to body to avoid thrashing. Boat the fish or place on a fish stringer (shark free areas). A stringer through the eyes (not halibut) will kill the fish. Uncock gun before exiting the water. Store gun upright or horizontal and never lean it up against anything. Gut and place fish on ice ASAP. Be a hunter, not a killer. Take only what you need and practice conservation. "Blue Water Hunting and Freediving" by Terry Mass is excellent on the subject.

KELP DIVING

Kelp comes in many varieties, but kelp diving refers to giant kelp. Giant kelp (Macrocystis Pyrifera) is the largest and fastest growing marine plant (algae) on earth. Growth can exceed 2 feet per day and reach over 80 feet high. Kelp thrives in cool clean water and is an indicator of a healthy environment. Kelp is secured by a holdfast which grabs a rock and is suspended by small gas-filled bladders at the base of the fronds (leaves). Kelp is high in iodine and is used in a variety of products. It's harvested by a large water lawn mower which trims several feet off the top (no commercial harvesting at Catalina). Underwater, a kelp bed resembles an enchanted forest and is home to diverse marine life. Diving the kelp beds is easy when a few skills are mastered. Practice snorkeling around the kelp bed. Discover the open channels that wind through the canopy. Use slow deliberate movements and be aware of the surroundings. Touch, smell and taste it (yummy!). Pull and stretch it like a rubber band. Roll and wrap in it like a sea otter, then relax and feel it loosen. Swim over the canopy using a small flutter kick while pushing the kelp under the body with the arms (kelp crawl).

Before diving, take compass bearings for underwater navigation. Observe the kelp signs to determine reef size, visibility and current. Streamline and tuck loose gear to prevent entanglements. Keep gear off arms and legs. Place knife inside leg, secure octopus regulator, trim excess straps, turn fin straps in (or tape) and tuck the console inside the buoyancy compensator. Be aware of hanging objects such as cameras and spearguns. Don't jump off the boat into the canopy, wait for an opening.

Diving under kelp is easier due to greater spacing. "Dive with the flow and watch where you go" to avoid entanglements. Getting caught is normal and seems to happen at the most inconvenient time. Don't panic, flail or twist. Stay calm, take a deep breath, it's no problem. First sign is movement restricted by a tugging feeling (usually tank valve or fin buckle). Just relax, reach back and untangle it. Kelp is very elastic so don't pull on it. Bend and give a quick jerk to snap the kelp. If all else fails, get a buddy to help, slowly use a knife to cut the kelp or remove the entangled equipment. Keep at least 500 PSI air in reserve to navigate out of the kelp bed. To surface inside the bed, locate a gap in the canopy and use exhaust bubbles to expand the opening or use arms to part the kelp. To descend, exhaust the BC and drop down feet first. On the surface it's often easier to swim around the kelp or use the kelp crawl to go over. Catalina's best diving is in and around the kelp, so get used to it and have fun.

KAYAK DIVING

Kayak diving offers many advantages. Launched from the beach or a boat, kayaks provide a platform and extend diving range. Many types of kayaks are available so choose one that fits your requirements. Narrow kayaks are faster (good for free divers). A wider kayak is slower, more stable and holds more equipment (good for Scuba divers). Some have compartments for equipment storage and moulded space for a tank.

Practice kayak techniques in calm water, without dive gear. Try launching, tipping and beaching. Observe the techniques of an experienced kayak diver. Assume you will tip over. Secure hatches, lash all gear and use safety lines. Put some air in the BC. If possible, put the tank in the bow when going out through surf and in the stern when coming in. The weight belt can go under your legs (weight centered and easy access). Before launching, observe the sea conditions and weather. Time the wave sets, paddle quickly and go straight into the waves. Use a paddle leash through the surf. If you get sideways, chances of dumping increase. If a wave is about to break over you, lean forward at the last moment and recover as quickly as possible, straighten the kayak and paddle hard. Try not to panic. Once through the surf zone, relax, catch your breath, re-secure and inventory your gear. Pace yourself. Use a steady paddling stroke to the dive site. Protect yourself from the sun and weather (sunscreen, hat, sunglasses, windbreaker, water and a snack). A waterproof box or dry sack can carry a VHF radio, flares, equipment spares and tools etc.

Once on site, anchor using a small (6-8 lb.) collapsible anchor, about 6' of chain and 180' of braided 1/4" line. A 2 to 1 scope (line to depth ratio) will work in calm conditions, or use more if greater wind or current. Hoisting the dive flag on a small 3' pole will help keep boaters away and make it easier to locate the kayak after the dive. If tired prior to dive, rest. Ready to dive, secure paddle and all loose gear. Put on mask, fins and snorkel and roll in gently to avoid tipping boat. Grab tank, BC and finally weight belt. Drop lines make gear retrieval easier (don't use for weight belt). Dive down to the anchor to insure good hold and easy retrieval.

After the dive, remove and secure the weight belt, tank, BC and any accessories. To get back in use the technique "BBF" (belly button - butt - feet). With one hand on each side of the kayak sides, kick up to point where belly button is centered, then twist and sit in seat and finally pull legs and feet up. Now relax, drink some liquid and have a snack. Secure and tuck in all loose lines. Pace yourself during the paddle back. Time the waves before going through the surf. Paddle fast and stay perpendicular to shore. If you dump, avoid getting pinned between the kayak and sand or tangled in loose lines. When you hit the beach, get out quickly (both legs exit on same side), grab the bow, lift and pull kayak up and out. Rinse all gear ASAP.

SHARK DIVING

Shark diving has become very popular at Catalina. This is deep blue water diving, often miles from the Island near the banks and rises. Sea lions, mola mola (giant ocean sunfish) and whales also frequent this realm. Several local and mainland charters are available. Most have a steel or aluminium shark cage as a safety device. The cage is suspended in the water with floats attached to the top and a line to the boat . Mid to late summer (Aug. to Nov.) is the best time and plan on a full day trip. Prior to the dive, check your gear (cameras, lights, batteries and film). After stowing gear, sit back and enjoy the ride. Boat procedures vary so listen to the divemaster's instructions. Birds or bait fish activity often indicates what's below. Once on site, the cage is dropped into the water and chumming begins. Chum is mashed up oily fish (usually mackerel) that is put over the side to create a fish oil slick and send chunks down through the water column. a bait cage or fish on a line will draw them from lower depths. Sharks move up and down in depth searching for food (use smell, electromagnetic and sound?). Also, low frequency sound (imitating a wounded fish) can be transmitted through a hydrophone to attract sharks. Over fishing and gill nets have reduced the number of sharks, so relax, it may take hours before they appear (bait and wait). When the first sharks appear (usually small blue sharks), slip quietly into the water. A splash may scare the sharks away. It's exciting to be with these beautiful creatures but try to stay as calm as possible, using slow deliberate movements. If this is your first encounter, swim directly over to the cage (your reference point for the dive). Learn to be comfortable in blue water (buoyancy control is essential). The boat is not anchored so good swimming ability helps. Most sharks approach from down current following the chum trail. Controlled feeding will keep the sharks in the area (too much may cause a frenzy). Sharks tend to become more active as their numbers increase. They generally attack prey from below and may be attracted to flashy metals and colors (especially orange). Don't ack like food. Sharks are sensitive to touch and may flee if grabbed. Electromagnetic fields of strobes or video camcorders may cause a quick reaction or bumping, so photographers stay alert.

Blue sharks (pg 106) are the most common shark observed off Catalina. Long, sleek and graceful, cruising at 2-3 M.P.H. in the upper 200 feet, these slow movers (low riders) seem curious and unafraid of divers. Blues are fairly predictable but not to be taken for granted (may bump or nip at times). A sudden disappearance of blues may signal the arrival of a mako.

Mako (shortfin) or bonito sharks (pg 136) are fast, active and ballistic like swimmers. They are similar in shape to the great white, are very toothy, unpredictable and can have an attitude. Makos may feed on blue shark pups.

Thresher sharks (pg 137) are fast and easily recognized by its long tail (equal to the length of its' body). The tail should be considered dangerous. Great white, hammerhead and ocean white tip sharks are out there, but rare. After the dive, you will have new tales to tell of an experience that most people only see on TV.

Fishing gear basics

1. Get the best fishing gear you can afford (fewer problems, less maintenence and longer life).
2. Basic outfit for Catalina is a 7 to 8 foot, single piece, medium to light action rod, with conventional high speed reel and 15-30 lb mono line.
3. Bottom and trolling outfit is a 5 1/2 to 6 1/2 foot single piece rod with roller tip with conventional reel and 300 to 500 yards of 50 to 80 lb mono or braided line.
4. Tackle box with assorted hooks, sinkers, swivels and clippers (saves teeth).
5. Bait tank or receiver and cooler with ice.

V. FISHING INFORMATION

Information on fishing knots, making bait and securing bait to hooks.

Fishing rules and regulations are often changing. Consult California Fish and Game rules and regulations. Regulations and updates can be accessed at their web site. www.dfg.ca.gov

FISHING KNOTS

Palomar Knot: Used to join fishing line to hooks, snaps, swivels and lures.

Double line (about 5") and pass loop through eye (hook, swivel, lure).

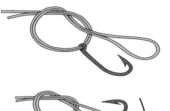

Tie loose overhand knot in doubled line with hook hanging from bottom.

Hold the overhand knot between thumb and forefinger and pass loop over hook, swivel or lure.

Pull the standing line and the bitter end together onto eye to tighten. Trim the bitter end.

Dropper Loop: Used to put loop in middle of a line.

Form a loop in the line at the desired location. Pull line from one side of loop down and pass it through and around that side of loop, keeping a thumb and forefinger in the new opening which is formed.

Push bottom of original loop up through new opening and hold with teeth. Wet knot and pull both ends in opposite directions.

Pull ends of line firmly until coils tighten and loop stands out from line.

Surgeon's End Loop: Used to put loop in the end of a line.

Double end of the line about 6" and tie a loose overhand knot.

Pinch the knot and bring the loop through ovehand knot once more.

Pull loop while holding standing line and bitter end. Tighten knot slow and even to desired sized loop. Trim the bitter end to about 1/8".

Albright Knot: Used to join fishing lines (monofilament or wire) of different diameters.

Bend a loop in end of the heavy line and pinch with left hand. Insert the bitter end of the light line through loop.

Pinch bitter end of light line tightly against the heavier strands of the loop. Wrap the light line over itself and continue wrapping around all three strands toward the round end of loop. Take at least 12 turns.

Insert bitter end of light line through end of loop. Ends must leave the loop on same side.

Still holding the heavier line, slide the coils of light line towards end of loop to 1/8" from end of loop. Use pliers to pull bitter end of light line tight while keeping coils from slipping off loop. Pull on the standing part of the lighter line. Pull the bitter end and standing part a second time. Pull both standing parts (heavy mono and light line) to tighten. Trim both tag ends.

MAKING & HOOKING BAIT

For most Catalina gamefish, natural bait is more effective than artificial bait or lures.Live bait is best, then fresh dead (on ice), before frozen. Bait can be bought fresh (Avalon Bait Barge pg 21), or frozen, or you can make your own live bait. Live bait is kept fresh and ready to use in a bait tank or bait receiver. Check frozen bait for freezer burn. Bait presentation is the key, hide hooks when posible and change bait as needed (almost every time a fish is caught).

Deepbody anchovy (Anchoa compressa) & California (Northern) anchovy: (Engraulis mordaxa): Also called chovies. Light tan colored with light band along body. Length to 6 inches. Handle carefully and try to keep the scales intact. Use the most active bait. Anchovies with a greenish hue (greenies) are best. To fish, hook on a short shanked live bait hook. Hook size determined by bait size and line size. Nose hook pinheads on a #6-8 hook with 10-15 lb test. Hook medium bait a #2-4 hook and large ones on a 1/0-2/0 hook with 15-30 lb test. For surface fishing, insert hook through outer edge of gill plate. For deeper fishing, use a sinker. Deeper swimming bait can be hooked through the anal fin. Frozen and fresh dead chovies hook the same or insert hook through bottom and top lip. Cutting frozen bait will release more scent. Cut in half, split cut each half and hook through lips or tail.

Topsmelt (Atherinops affinis): Length to 15 inches. To catch, use micro jig fly gangions or "Lucky Joe's". To fish, hook same a anchovy. For 8-1 in bait use #2/0-3/0 short shank bait hook. If bait is too fast, clip the fins.

Pacific mackerel (Scomber japonicus): Also called greenback. Body is tapered at both ends. Head and back are dark blue with about 30 wavy, vertical, dark green stripes. Length to 25 inches (6.3 lbs). They spawn March - May. Voracious indiscriminant feeders. To catch, use a small piece of cut bait (anchovy or squid) on a #2-6 hook. Lures work or use a micro jig fly gangion with a 1-2 oz, chrome, torpedo sinker to help it sink. They are a scrapy little fighter. To fish, hook the bait on a #4/0-7/0 short shank bait hook or #1/0-3/0 trebble hook through the two nasal pores or hook under the anal fin, or hook in back of

Sardine (Sardinops sagax): Length to 15 inches. Thought to be overfished and once on verge of extinction, sardines have made a comeback. To fish, hook same as anchovy or use #1/0-3/0 trebble hook in dorsal or anal fin.
Brown and junk baits are a mess of other small fishes (shiner perch, tom cod, queenfish, etc...) used as bait.
Squid (Loligo opalescens): Long pointed body (arrow sahaped) with triangular fins. Spawn late October through April, but usually appear beginning December. Lays 4 inch white, tube like, eggs on bottom. Length to 10 inches. Catching squid (squidding) is best accomplished at night. Squid are attracted to light. Use high powered lights, hung over the boat and pointed directly at the water and wait for squid to float up. Squid may

not rise to the surface. Use brail nets or jigging to capture. For jigging, you need a limber rod to feel the bite. Drop squid jig to the bottom, reel it up a few inches then slowly pull it up (about 3 feet). Once up, let it drop slowly, squid will bite as the jig falls. Don't allow any slack in your line or you won't feel the bite. When the rod tip lifts up a little while your are lowering your jig, a squid is nibbling at your lure. When you feel the nibble, set the hook (multi spiked barbless) by gently jerking up on your rod. If the hook does not set, don't give up, keep jigging. Squid may nibble the lure several times, giving you several chances to hook the same squid. Fresh squid (calimari) can also make a fine meal. Most gamefish love to eat squid. To fish, hook through the tail with a 3/0 bait hook about one hook length from the pointed end) or hook through the eye. Frozen squid hook the same but work better if jigged to simulate live squid. Squid is tough, holds onto hooks well and makes excellent cut bait. Cut long or diagonal strips and work similar to whole squid. Strips can also be added to lures to increase effectivness. Tentacles are even tougher and used similar to strip bait. Every few years, larger squid (Dosidicus gigas) apear. Length to 50 inches. Whole they are used as bait for mako shark and swordfish. Long cut strips are good bait. Caugh fresh, this large calimari is good for eating.
California grunion (Leuresthes tenuis): Also called smelt. Length to 7.5 inches (average 4-6 inches). Spawn from March to August. A grunion run is spectacular
as thousands of the small silvery fish wash ashore at high tide. Stranded, the female digs into the sand and lays eggs while the male wraps around and fertilizes her. They may only be caught by hand, so grab a 5 gallon bucket and hit the beach. This fish can also be eaten fresh sauteed in butter or batter. Frozen grunion can be fished similar to anchovy as whole on a #1/0-4/0 bait hook or as cut bait. Check Fish and Game grunion web page (w,dfg.ca.gov/mrd/gruschd.html) for closures and information.

FISHING RIGS

Use the best quality new line. Light as posible for maximum deception, but strong enough to do the job. Hooks should be sharp and shiny. Hook size is determined by bait size and size of fish you're after.

Fly lining rig: Used for kelp bass.

Hook is tied directly to the end of main fishing line with no weight attached. Used for maximum bait movement. A small line sinker can be attached to work bait down in water column.

Drift (sliding sinker) rig: Used for halibut and white seabass.

1 to 2 1/2 (1/2 to 2) oz slide weights. Use 1 or two sliding egg sinkers above a swivel and a leader on the other end. A sliding barrel swivel up the main line and then tie another barrel swivel to the main line. A torpedo sinker (heavy 8-12 oz) with 8-10 inches of leader to the sliding barrel swivel, then attach leader to the other end of the swivel that was attached to the main line. Hook bait through nose or for dead bait, through lower jaw into nose (pg 98).

15-30 lb test line.

1/2 to 3 oz sliding egg weights (single or double).

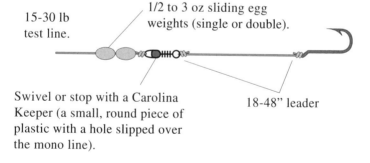

Swivel or stop with a Carolina Keeper (a small, round piece of plastic with a hole slipped over the mono line).

18-48" leader

Marlin live bait rig: Will allow leader to be reeled up and cast out.

30 lb mono line

80 lb mono line 10-12 ft

80 lb mono line 10-12 ft

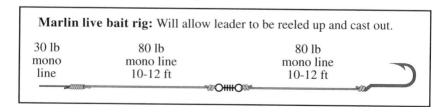

Dropper loop rig: Refered to as a gangnion. Variations used for rockfish, sanddabs and yellowtail (spring). As a surf rig, toss out, leave on bottom then reel in steady. It's important the gangnion is tied correctly. No angles, no tangles!

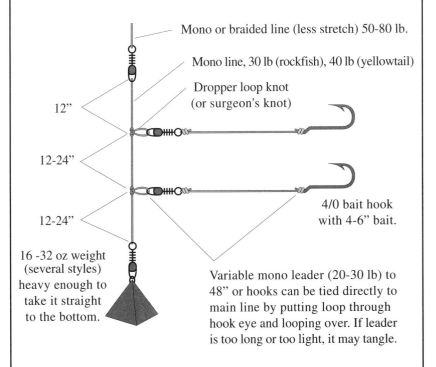

Mono or braided line (less stretch) 50-80 lb.

Mono line, 30 lb (rockfish), 40 lb (yellowtail)

Dropper loop knot
(or surgeon's knot)

12"

12-24"

12-24"

4/0 bait hook
with 4-6" bait.

16 -32 oz weight
(several styles)
heavy enough to
take it straight
to the bottom.

Variable mono leader (20-30 lb) to
48" or hooks can be tied directly to
main line by putting loop through
hook eye and looping over. If leader
is too long or too light, it may tangle.

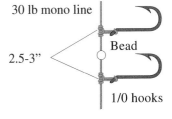

30 lb mono line

2.5-3"

Bead

1/0 hooks

Sanddab rigs are variations that can use more lines and hooks. The shorter the gangnion and more hooks (about 8), the better. Hooks are looped on and not tied, by putting dropper loop through hook eye and looping over. One or two beads can be placed between hooks (may help).

**Check Fish and Game regulations for type of rig
allowed for different fish.**

VI. MARINE LIFE

Information on marine plants, algae, fish,
sharks, shellfish and more.

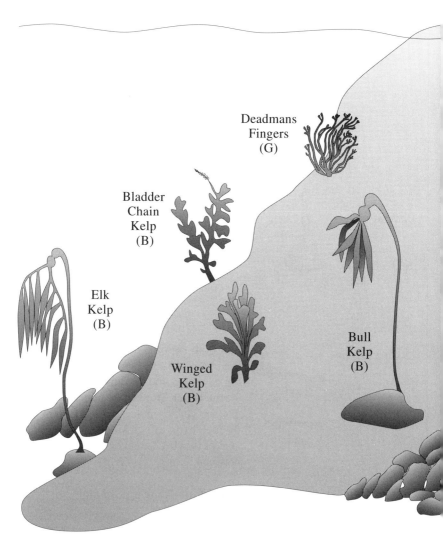

Deadmans
Fingers
(G)

Bladder
Chain
Kelp
(B)

Elk
Kelp
(B)

Bull
Kelp
(B)

Winged
Kelp
(B)

MARINE PLANTS & ALGAE (Plantae)

Most of the plants encountered by divers are algae. Algae is divided into groups by color. Green algae (Chlorophyta) is green colored, small to medium in size and mostly found in intertidal water (G). Red algae (Phaeophyta) is reddish colored and may display purple, yellow, green or brown shades (R). Brown algae (Rhodophyta) is brown colored, largest of all algae and abundant off the California coast (B). Sea grasses (Trachaeophyta) are among the few plants, eel and surf grasses that inhabit the shallow water (P).

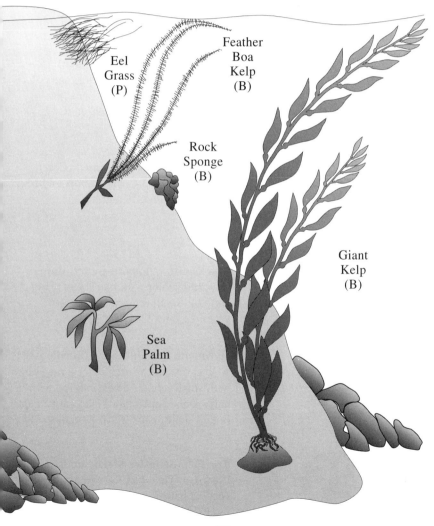

Eel
Grass
(P)

Feather
Boa
Kelp
(B)

Rock
Sponge
(B)

Giant
Kelp
(B)

Sea
Palm
(B)

FISH (Osteichthyes)

Blue-banded goby (Lythrypnus dalli): Bright red-orange body with 2 to 6 bright blue stripes. Small sharp teeth. Hides in small crevices. Can change sex from female to male and back again (hermaphrodite) Length to 2.5".

Giant kelpfish (Heterostichus rostratus): Long snout, body and dorsal fin with forked tail. Brown to gold color varies to match background (shape and color similar to blade of kelp). Found shallow to 130 ft deep. Length to 24".

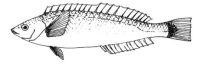

Senorita (Oxyjulis californica): Cigar-shaped with yellow-orange color and black spot at tail. Cleaner fish. Found to 330 ft deep. Length to 12".

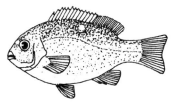

Opaleye (Girella nigricans): Green-blue color with 1-2 white spots on back. Fish year round. Length to 25".

Blacksmith (Chromis punctipinnis): Dark blue color with black spots at back and tail. Small mouth. Length to 12".

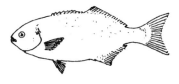

Halfmoon (Medialuna californiensis): Also called Blue perch. Blue-gray color with small mouth. Sleek looking with half moon shaped tail. Fish year round. Found shallow to 130 ft. Length to 18".

Treefish (Sebastes nigrocinctus): Rockfish. Yellow color with dark vertical bars on yellow body and reddish, pink lips. Length to 16".

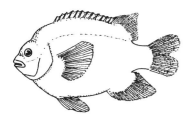

Garibaldi (Hypsypops rubicundus): California State Marine Fish (protected). Bright orange color. Very territorial when guarding nest (March - October). Small juveniles have bright blue spots. Length to 14".

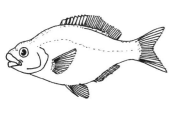

Rubberlip surfperch (Rhacochilus toxotes): Brassy brown color. Distinguished by large thick lips. Found shallow to 150 ft deep. Length to 18".

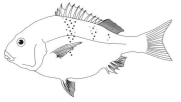

Sargo (Anisotremus davidsonii): Member of the grunt family. Silvery body with dark vertical bar extending from dorsal fin down past pectoral fin. May have lighter bars toward tail. Found around reefs and kelp beds. Depth to 130 ft deep. Length to 17.5".

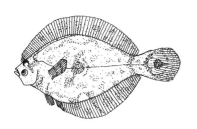

C-O turbot (Pleuronichthys coenosus): Lives on sand or rock bottom. Body is rounded, mottled grayish-brown on top with 2 distinctive marks on tail. White on bottom. Round bug-eyes. Usually caught incidentally. Spawn Mar-Aug. Found shallow to 966 ft deep. Length to 14".

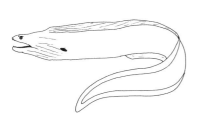

California moray eel (Gymnothorax mordax): Green to mottled brown color. Live in rocky caves and crevices. Have sharp teeth, a good sense of smell and poor eyesight. Avoid sticking hands in holes and carrying game. Found shallow to 130 ft deep. Length to 60".

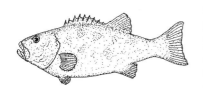

Giant (Black) sea bass (Stereolepis gigas): Protected fish can live over 100 years. Only 2 spines on gill cover. Juveniles may have dark spots on side (spots fade and blend with age). Length to 84". Weight to 557 pounds.

SHARKS & RAYS (Chondrichthyes)

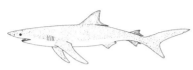

Blue shark (Prionace glauca): Lives in open ocean. Long pointed nose. Electric blue/gray back with silver/gray belly. Camoflauged from above and below. Long, pointed, pectoral fins and swept back tail. Have sharp teeth. Be aware when carrying bloody fish. Avoid contact. See shark diving (pg. 94). Length to 156" (avg 24 to 70").

Leopard shark (Trakis semifasciata): Lives on sand and mud bottoms. Gray with large dark spots and cross bars on back. Length to 83" .

Swell shark (Cephaloscyllium ventriosum): Lives on the bottom, in caves and crevices. Mottled brown color with dark brown spots and plump belly. Can inflate its stomach to swell in size when disturbed or caught. Female lays amber colored egg cases. Length to 45".

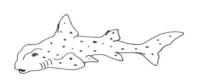

Horn shark (Heterodontus francisci): Lives on bottom in crevices and caves. Brown with small to large dark spots. Rounded horns (ridge) over eyes on head. Sharp spine in front of each dorsal fin. Female lays olive green corkscrew (spiral-shaped) egg cases in crevasses. Length to 48".

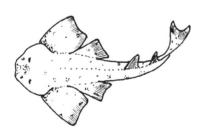

Pacific angel shark (Squatina californica): Flattened, territorial shark, lives on sand and mud bottoms (partially buried). Large head with mouth on underside and broad, expanded, pectorial fins (wings) covered with brown spots. Length to 60".

Pacific electric ray (Torpedo californica): Also called Torpedo ray. Large round head and body. Mottled grayish-brown color. Lives on mud or sand bottom or may be free swimming. Can be aggressive and deliver up to 80 volts electric charge. Avoid contact. Length to 55".

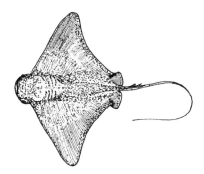

Bat ray (Myliobatis californica): Lives on sand and mud bottoms. Large, raised, blunt head with pointed tail and stinger. Eats clams and crustaceans. Length to 60" (body width is about the same as length).

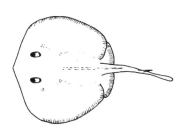

Round stingray (Urolophus halleri): Lives on sand and mud bottoms. Large blunt head with round body and sharp barbs on tail. Brown on top and white-yellow belly. Avoid contact (shuffle feet when walking on sand bottom). If lacerated (usually in calf or ankle) immerse in hot water. Length to 22".

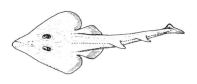

Shovelnose guitarfish (Rhinobatus productus): Lives on sand bottoms in shallow water. Shape similar to guitar with single row of spines and long tail. Length to 65".

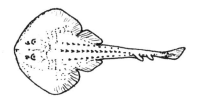

Thornback (Platyrhinoidis triseriata): Lives on sand and mud bottoms. Three rows of small spines on back and tail. Two dorsal fins on tail. Length to 36".

SHELLFISH (Mollusca)

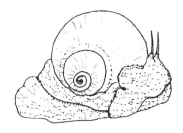

Lewis moon snail (Polinices lewisii):
Lives on sand or mud. Thick, smooth,
tan shell shaped like a ball. Giant-sized
grayish foot. Lays eggs in a sand
encrusted collar, same diameter as
shell. Diameter to 6 in.

Smooth turban (Norrisia norrisii):
Also called Norris topsnail. Smooth
reddish-brown shell with pearl white
inside. Green spot on underside of
shell. Foot is black with orange rim
Found on kelp and brown algae. Found
intertidal to 100 ft. Height to 2 in.

Wavy turban snail (Astraea undosa):
Shell has wavy spiral ridge, ornate
markings and covered by a brown skin
and marine growth. Inside shell is pearl
white. Lives on rock and sand bottoms.
Used as food by the Pimu (Native
Islanders). Height to 5 in.

**Leafy hornmouth (Ceratostoma
foliatum):** Brown and white colored,
often banded. Three, leaf like, winged
extentions. Found in rocky kelp areas.
Length to 4 in.

**Giant keyhole limpet (Megathura
crenulata):** Lives on rocky reefs.
Shield shaped shell with oval hole.
Body is brown mottled to black and
often covers shell. Foot is similar to
abalone. Length to 7 in.

Kellet's welk (Kelletia kelletii):
Lives on rocks, gravel and sand. Thick white to tan colored, spiral shell with prominent nodes. Very common at Catalina. Used as food by the Pimu (Native Islanders). Length to 8 in.

Mussel (Mytilus californianus):
Lives in shallow water, tightly attached to rocks and pilings etc... Purple, gray-black shell covered with a black skin. Mussels are quarantined between May 1 to Oct 31 due to feeding on toxic organisms. Length to 10 in.

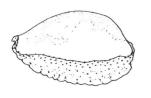

Chestnut cowry (Cypraea spadicea):
Only cowry found on California coast. Found on rocks in clear wateers. Smooth glossy shell with white sides and brown patch on top. Bumpy reddish-brown mantle may cover shell. Retracted for protection. Length to 3 in.

Green abalone (Haliotis fulgens):
Protected. Oval flat-shaped shell with 5 to 7 slightly raised holes. Reddish brown to dark green color. Long olive green tentacles. Some marine growth on shell. Found in shallow water (5-60 ft). Many abalone (mostly black) died of withered foot disease Length to 9 in.

Pink abalone (Haliotis corrugata):
Protected. Deep round shell with wavy ridges and 2 to 6 volcano-like holes. Dull red color with corrugated edge. Inside is pearly green/pink. Lacy black and white (peppered) tentacles. More marine growth on shell. Found in deeper water (5-120 ft). Length to 8 in.

OCTOPUS (Cephalopoda)

Two spotted octopus (Octopus bimaculatus): Can change color and texture. Very intelligent. Found hiding in crevices and other objects. Look for shell fragments outside of den. Length to 36" (usually less than 12").

SEA SLUGS (Opisthobranchia)

Sea Hare (Aplysia californica): Mollusc with no shell. Mottled brown to olive to dark purple in color. 2 flaps on back and 2 tentacle-like appendages on head (Similar to rabbit). Lives in rocky and sandy areas. Length to 18".

Spanish shawl (Flabellinopsis iodenea): Nudibranch with bright purple body and bright orange, hairlike appendages on back. Found on rocky reefs. Length to 2".

CRABS, SHRIMPS & BARNACLES (Crustacea)

Sheep crab (Loxorhynchus grandis): Oval shaped body with long legs. Gray to tan color. Often covered with marine growth. Length to 70".

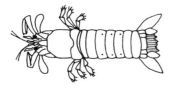

Mantis shrimp (Pseudosquilla bigelowi): Purplish color with band on back. Tail similar to lobster. Dangerous razor sharp appendage. Eyes articulate independently (wide field of view)and see infrared. Live in well manicured (shell and pebble entrance) holes on sandy bottom. Length to 8".

Barnacle (Balanus spp.): Secured to rocks and pilings. Sharp cutting edges. Avoid contact. Diameter to 1".

STARFISH, CUCUMBERS & URCHINS
(Echinodermata)

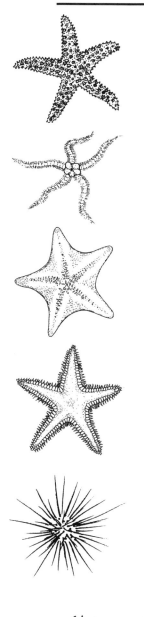

Giant-spined star (Pisaster giganteus): Randomly spaced, white tipped spines with blue ring at base. Lives on rocky reefs. Length to 22".

Brittle star (Ophiuroidea spp.): Found under rocks. Wide range of types and sizes. Diameter to 6".

Sea bat (Patiria miniata): Thick arms with webbing between. Scaled surface can be various shades of red, orange, brown, purple or green. Yellowish underside. Often in large numbers. Lives on rocky reefs, sand or mud bottoms. Diameter to 6".

Spiny sand star (Astropecten armatus): Tannish-gray color. Arms bordered by row of plates. Lives on sand or mud bottom. Diameter to 10".

Sea urchin (Strongylocentrotus spp.): Giant red urchin is red to dark purple color with long spines (dia. to 7"); Purple urchin is smaller (dia. to 3"). Lives in shallow reefs and may burrow into rock. Spines may puncture skin and break off (very painful). If stuck, remove spines and fragments. Avoid contact.

California sea cucumber (Parastichopus parvimensis): Reddish-brown in color. Bumpy surface with tube feet. Length to 18".

ANEMONES & JELLYFISH (Cnidaria)

Giant green anemone (Anthopleura xanthogrammica): Deep to pale green color (white in crevices). Lives in mid to low tidal areas attached to rocks and crevices. Diameter to 6".

Tube anemone (Pachycerianthus fimbriatus): Dark bumpy tube. Long whip-like tentacles in a wide range of colors. Size to 12" high and 2" diameter.

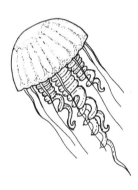

Purple striped jellyfish (Pelagia panopyra): White translucent body with purple radial markings. Live at the surface and mid water. Stinging tentacles become shorter and thicker with age. Carefully clean the affected area. Use of vinegar may help. Length to 140" and 24" diameter.

SPONGES (Porifera)

Gray Moon Sponge (Spheciospongia confoederata): Smooth gray sponge with moon-like craters on outer ridge. Attached to rocks usually 40 to 60 ft deep. Length to 450 cm.

VII. GAME

Basic information on how to identify, catch, clean and cook
lobster, scallops and fish (spearfishing and angling).

Fish and Game size and limits change and are not
included in game information.
Always consult current regulations.
www.dfg.ca.gov
Practice conservation (catch, photograph and release).

SCALLOPS

Purple-hinged rock scallop (Crassadoma gigantea): Typically an irregular, oval spiny, brownish orange top shell, often covered with heavy marine growth. Scallops are bivalves (two shells). Unlike other scallops, the right valve is cemented to rock, Inside shell is white with a purple hinge connecting the two valves. The two halves are opened and shut by the adductor muscle (edible portion) which opens and closes the left valve. When open the mantle is exposed. The mantle has tentacles and color is pink/orange or gray/olive green (fewer). Length to 8" (usually less than 6").

Natural History: Scallops begin as free swimming larvae (1/300") then, at 1/16 to 1/8", atattach to rocks or pilings by temporary byssal threads. If threads break free, swimming may help find a new home. Once attached, they begin to cement (1/2 to 1"), conforming to the occupied terrain. They grow about 2 inches per year and take about 3 years to reach harvest size. Scallops are filter feeders and rely on prevailing and tidal currents to bring them food. They eat phytoplankton (mostly dinoflagellates). Sexes are generally separate and spawning occurs twice yearly in late spring to early summer and mid fall. Few predators are able to penetrate the hard spiny shell.

Diving for scallops is like an Easter egg hunt, the hard part is trying to find them. Half the shell is cemented to rock so they're easy to catch. There is no commercial taking of rock scallops so only sport diving or collecting along shore is allowed. Scallops tend to shy away from direct sunlight by attaching to pinnacles, cracks, crevicees, cliff faces, overhangs and outcroppings. They range in depth from shallow to over 90 feet. Rock scallops are masters of camouflage. Looking like rocks and encrusted by marine growth, they blend into their surroundings. Scallops tend to be on the side of the reef exposed to the prevailing current which brings microscopic food. They are often found near the entrance to bays. Filter feeding requires the scallop to open its shell (lips) slightly (about 1/2 inch) exposing the mantle or "scallop smile". The orange or green smile, contrasted against the marine background, provides the best way to spot them. Scan the area forward while kicking easily. Searching for scallops requires good buoyancy control and a smooth silent approach. Avoid touching the rocks. Scallops will close if a shadow crosses or the water vibrations surrounding them is disturbed. When a scallop is spotted, note the location, if they close, they can hide right in front of your face. Before removing look for other scallops as they tend to come in groups. To remove, slip a heavy knife, ab iron or large screwdriver between where the shell is cemented to the rock and pry off. Gloves are a must. Removal requires a little expertise, scallops can vary from easy to almost impossible. Avoid spending too much time on difficult scallops.

There is no size limit, but scallops smaller than palm (button about 1/5 size of shell) size are not worth the effort. Current daily bag limit is 10 (check F & G regulations for updates). Collecting scallops is like putting rocks into the game bag (10 to 15 lbs), so be aware of buoyancy changes. Some divers use a thin bladed knife to slip in between the shells and remove only the innards. This technique, called cleaning (see pg, 110), affords more protection to the ecosystem, but is difficult and time consuming. Cleaners often use a plastic bag to hold the meat, avoiding the heavy game bag. Beware, if the scallop is cut in half, Fish and Game will count them as two scallops. Scallops are easier to clean on the surface and will stay fresh for several hours on surface. Some divers eat the button fresh from the shell, either underwater or on the surface. There is no closed season for scallops which provides a year-round game of hide and seek. The diver who wins this game is rewarded with a very tasty meal. Always practice conservation. Harvest where abundant and leave enough to reproduce.

Typical scallop locations

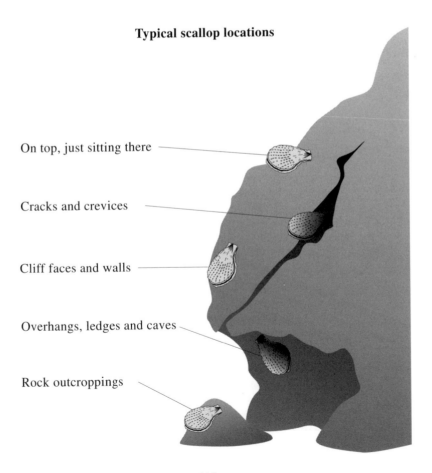

On top, just sitting there

Cracks and crevices

Cliff faces and walls

Overhangs, ledges and caves

Rock outcroppings

SCALLOP CLEANING

The object is to get the adductor muscle (button) away form the shell.

Scallops can be difficult to open when shut tight and several methods are possible. Lay them all out and wait, slowly some will begin to open. There is a small opening on one side that can be used. A single broom bristle or few drops of tabasco in the hole may irritate it to open. Inserting a screwdriver and twisting may force it apart or try chipping off the shell edge. When possible, slip a long thin knife between the shells , then scrape the muscle (button) from the flat shell and pull the shell halves apart.

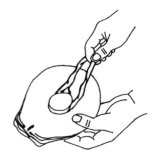

With the button still attached to the shell half, use fingers and knife edge to remove the viscera and mantle (guts). Guts should come off in one piece. Do not eat the guts as they may contain contaminants.

Scrape the button away from the shell.

Trim the small, hard, white portion (edible) from the button. Scrape or scrub off any remaining brown (guts) and rinse. Many like to eat the meat raw from the shell. Best eaten ASAP. Will keep in refridgerator up to 24 hours.

SCALLOP COOKING

Rock scallops have a sweet nutty flavor and are considered best of all scallops. Cook until the meat is opaque (don't overcook).

Scallop scampi

Scallops: Rinsed, patted dry and cut into 1/4 pieces.
Garlic: One clove minced
Onion: 3 tablespoons minced   Lemon juice: 1 teaspoon
Tarragon: 2 teaspoons minced   Unsalted butter: 3 tablespoons

Directions: Heat 1-1/2 T. butter over medium high heat. Sauté scallops about 1 minute then remove. Add other ingredients and cook until onion is soft. Replace scallops and cook until heated through. Good over pasta.

Scallop kabobs

Scallops: Large ones cut in half.
Skewers: Metal or wood (soak in water 1-2 hours).
Bell peppers, onions, mushrooms, cherry tomatoes etc...
Basting sauce: Soy with a little ginger, garlic & lemon.

Directions: Place scallops and vegetables on skewers. Place on hot oiled grill for about 4 minutes. Turn and baste with sauce.

Scalloperoni pizza

Scallops: thinly sliced.
Pizza crust: or french bread or "Boboli", etc...
Vegies: Onions, bell peppers, mushrooms, olives, etc...
Cheese: Mozzarella and parmesan.
Sauce: Pesto or tomato

Directions: Cover crust with sauce. Add vegetable toppings and cheese. Bake in oven until crust is brown. Remove and add scallop slices (lobster chunks are also tasty). Sprinkle on premising cheese. Replace in oven and cook about 6 to 8 minutes. This makes a little seafood go a long way.

LOBSTER

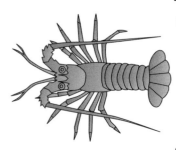

California Spiny Lobster (Panulirus interruptus): Also called bug. Hard red shell (body) with spines pointing forward and large curved spines line edge of tail. Length to 36" (24" lobster may weigh 15 pounds or more).

Natural history: From Dec - Mar the male deposits a gray paste (sperm spot) plastered on the stomach of the female. Spawning occurs from Mar - Aug. Females carry the eggs in spring and may release 50,000 (8") to 800,000 eggs into the currents in late summer. Few will survive the ten years required to reach legal size. Females have a special claw on rear leg to tend (preen) eggs and larger spines and flaps to cover and secure eggs. Lobster continue to grow throughout their life and may live 100 years. When lobster grow too big for their shell, they climb out and discard it (molt). Lobster molt about once each year, more often in early years and usually in summer. The soft, defenseless body will later become hard during this growing phase. Main defense is its hard spiny shell and the use of rapid tail thrusts to swim away backwards. Lobster have poor eyesight but have tiny sensory hairs, especially on antenae. They sense changes in light, water vibrations, touch, taste and chemical scents (smell). By day, lobster hide in caves and crevices and will usually "porch sit" near the entrance of a hole with antenna sticking out. Lobster are nocturnal scavengers that venture out at night, searching the bottom for scraps of food and will eat almost anything. Not usually migratory.

Diving: October through mid March is lobster season. A fishing license and 3 1/4 inch lobster measuring gauge are required. Measure from between spines on top of head tow where tail joins the body. Check F & G regulations for updates. Some special equipment will help. Divers can only take lobster by hand, so heavy flexible gloves are needed for protection from spines, bug bites and urchin spines etc ... For searching at night have a powerful, wide angle, underwater light and a back up or two (just in case). Head mounted lights can free up both hands. Check the batteries before diving and carry spares. Some divers attach a chemical light to tank valve. To store the many anticipated bugs, take a large, easy to open, game bag. Bags with special openings and cloth bags with mesh on bottom are good. Bug gauge can be attached to bag or light. Streamline any loose gear, roll up the bag, and tuck octopus, guages and fin straps prior to diving. A compass and navigation skills are helpful for search patterns . Know your gear by feel. Plan to dive at night from twilight to early morning. A night with little or no moon is best. The less dived areas tend to produce the most bugs. If possible, a recon dive during the day will help determine bug populations. Plan to be the first divers in the water and avoid other divers for greater success. Search the rocky reefs near kelp beds, surrounding sand and in shallow eel grass. Glide smoothly over and around the rocks while sweeping the light from side to side. Use good search patterns, covering a maximum area quick and throughly. Try shallow (often found less than 15 feet) and then go deeper. When bugs are sighted at a certain depth, concentrate efforts in that range. If none are sighted in a certain area, move somewhere else (hit and run). When a bug is spotted in the open, first estimate the size. Best to approach form behind or side. The antenna direction can show where its attention lies. Best if it's not focused on you. Avoid touching antenae which invokes an immediate response. A powerful light may stun the bug for a few seconds. Aim for the joint where the back (body) and tail meet. Surprise is the key, don't hesitate or one quick tail flip and it's gone. Try to pin the bug to the bottom then grab. Hold big bugs against chest. Bugs hide by day and often hide at night (experienced bug grabbers can bag them by day). Look for antenna, tails and legs in caves, holes, crevices, under ledges in kelp and eel grass. When the bug is in a hole, first check for urchins, eels and scorpionfish. Bugs are curious and may move out to check you out. Thrust hand into the top or side of the hole and grab the back or base of antenna (horns). If the bug gets wedged in the hole (locked up), a quick, violent, shaking may disorient and dislodge it. Teamwork can be effective by designating a bagger and catcher, then switching positions. Try not to blind buddy with light. A bug in a hole may have a back door for escape. This is a good place to position a second diver. Bugs that are difficult or too deep in a hole should be passed over (not worth the time). Bugs are fast and elusive. A good bug diver must be aggressive, dexterious, determined and prepared to get banged around in tight places and surf.

Fishing for lobster is done with a hoop net. A hoop net is a large metal ring with a net and line bridle (to pick up flat) secured to the rim. A line, long enough to reach from surface to bottom is attached to the bridle. A small float attached to the top of the bridle will keep bugs from being ejected during pull. Secure the bait (fish, chicken, can of cat food etc....) and lower to the bottom.

Be patient and allow time for the lobster to find the food (20 minutes or more). When ready, pull (fast as posible) to the surface and into the boat. **Once in hand**, hold on tight and measure across the back with the lobster gauge. Beware of the large spines that line the edge of the tail. Release bugs that are too small (shorts). Try to avoid breaking the legs and antenna of shorts which causes disability. If legal, roll up the tail and place in the bag tail first (if flips, swims into bag). Be careful, don't let other bugs escape. **Back on the boat**, re-measure your catch. Remember, be courteous and quiet to other boaters at night. Stay out of commercial lobster traps. Lobster fisherman are not allowed to trap the front side of the island and are just trying to make a living. Practice conservation, take only what's needed, leave the really big ones (great breeders), replace shorts in holes and replace any females with eggs. Good luck!

119

LOBSTER CLEANING

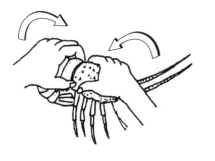

1. Remove the tail from the lobster body: Roll the tail in, then grab tail and body at carapace and twist in opposite directions and pull apart. Large bugs (over 4 lbs) have meat in horns and base of legs.

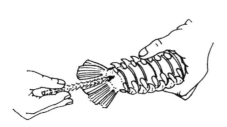

2. Remove the intestinal vein: Break off about 3/4 of one antenna. Stick the broken end of antennae in the anal hole. Push in, twist and pull out antenna. The spines will grab and remove the vein. Roll lobster tail and freeze if desired.

3. Split lobster tail lengthwise: Lay tail with back facing up. Carefully pierce back of shell with stiff knife and force down to split in half. Remove vein if not done prior.

Keep fresh: Live in receiver or game bag is best. Keep bugs cool. Bugs will stay alive in refridgerator overnight.
Freezing: Whole deveined tail (not split) is best frozen in water. After thawing; boil whole tail; BBQ or bake (1 lb/15 min) split tail; or remove meat from shell to skewer or fry.

LOBSTER COOKING

Grilled Lobster

Lobster: Tails cleaned and split in half lengthwise.
Herbs: Garlic, parsley, paprika,etc.
Butter and Lemon (even a little white wine)

Directions: Place tail halves, shell side down, on hot grill and cook about 8 - 10 minutes. Baste meat with butter to keep moist. Turn and cook about 6 - 8 minutes (don't overcook, meat is opaque when raw and turns white when done). Melt butter and add garlic and parsley (if desired). Glaze meat with melted butter and light sprinkle of paprika (perhaps a dash of tabasco). Serve hot with melted herb butter and lemon wedges.

Boiled Lobster

Lobster: Whole live or tail.

Directions: Drop whole live lobster or tail into boiling salt water. Size of lobster determines cooking time (1 lb / 8 minutes; 2 lbs / 12 minutes ; 3 to 5 lbs / 15 minutes; 6 lbs / 20 minutes). Cook until bright red (don't overcook).
Serve with melted butter and lemon wedges (see above).

Lobster Cocktail

Lobster
Cocktail sauce: Store bought, old family recipe or see page 121.
Celery
Lemon

Directions: Cook lobster (see boiled lobster). Let cool and refrigerate. Remove meat from shell and cut into small shredded chunks. Chop celery into fine pieces. Combine lobster, celery and cocktail sauce. Serve in small dishes and garnish with lemon wedges.

ROCKFISH, SCULPIN, LING COD & CABEZON

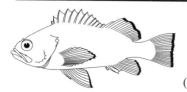

Rockfishes in general: 62 species of rockfish inhabit the California coast, the highest concentration in the world. All are members of the family Scorpaenidae (Scorpion fishes) and genus Sebastes. They are divided into two groups. Demersal rockfish stay close to the bottom and have bright colors and patterns. Many of these bottom species share the common name red snapper and rock cod. Pelagic rockfish school in the water column and are more uniformly colored in black, blue, brown or olive. Rockfish are found just beneath the surface to 1000 feet. Length is generally less than 24 inches (avg 10 to 18").

Natural history: In all rockfishes, fertilization is internal. Rockfish bear their young alive and are just under a quarter inch when they are released as helpless larvae into the water column. These larvae drift with the plankton and currents for 3-4 months. Juveniles then settle to the bottom, near shore, seeking shelter near structures (rocky reefs, crevices, caves, around breakwaters, sunken ships, piles of rubble and kelp beds). After one year they may grow to about 6 inches and then take another 15 years to reach 15 inches. Fish larger than 20 inches may be quite old. Although quite similar in appearance, each species develops different behavior characteristics and food preferences. Vermilion rockfish (S. miniatus) are nervous. Blue rockfish (S. mystinus) are usually found North of cental California, but also school over Farnsworth Bank. Kelp rockfish (S. atrovirens) seldom swim far from the kelp canopy. Most rockfish lay motionless on the bottom and are able to move quickly in bursts for defense and feeding. Diet consists of octopus, squids, small crustaceans, krill and small fishes such as anchovies, lanternfish, hake and other rockfish.

Spearfishing: A short, one or two banded gun, small pneumatic or pole spear (quickly reloaded) are easy to maneuver around rocky bottoms. Use a paralyzer head, trident, 5 pointed or rock point head for shooting small fish in rocky areas. These tips will often hit rock. A speedy reload will often make the difference between landing one fish or many. Look for a fish shaped outline among the rocks and kelp beds. They will normally let you get fairly close to them. Avoid looking the fish in the eye and approach at an angle rather than a direct path. There are many species of rockfish with may different characteristics. Some species of rockfish have been severely depleted. Be selective and take only what you need.

Fishing: Rockfish hit year round (best in summer) from depths shallow as 20 feet to over 1000 feet. Rockfish are not exactly known for their fighting ability, the skill is in the hunt and boat handling. You need good charts, a GPS and high quality fish finder and know how to use them. Several fishing charts are available for sale. First, you have to find a productive spot. Big fish can be found on and around the same offshore banks as tuna and sharks. A good rockfish "hole" will often produce several kinds of rockfishes. A nice calm morning is best. A 7-foot, all roller, trolling rod with a 6/0 Conventional reel and 80 pound Dacron line works. Electric reels are practical for fishing deep. Use a dropper loop rig (pg 101) with 1-2 baited hooks. above a sinker that is heavy enough to take it straight to the bottom. When fishing shallow, the rig can be downsized. The bait should be tough enough to remain firmly on the hook while being nibbled and chewed upon by the quarry. Live squid is the best bait then frozen is next best. Belly strips or pieces are another good bet, particularly for lingcod! Live anchovies, smelt, sardine, grunion, mussel, clam, crab and shrimp work well. Jigs and lures, bounced along the bottom, are less effective but may catch larger fish. Strips of bait and scents can be added to jig hook. Get set up on your spot and be ready to drop. Judge the wind, current and swell. Position your boat so it drifts over the spot or along the contour of the reef or shelf. When drifting perpendicular to the shelf or on a small hole, make several small drifts. You need to drop right on them, which is difficult when fishing deep water. It takes time to let down and haul up the rig. Time your drop to hit the hole. Let out line as fast as possible with thumb light on spool. Stop when you hit bottom then reel up a few turns (avoids hang-ups). Stay close to the bottom, but don't get stuck. Rockfish like active baits, so jig your baits or tug on the line between the reel and first guide. If there are fish, and they're hungry, you'll get bit! When you feel a strike, set the hook, then let settle till next strike and repeat before reeling in. Red colored rockfish, inhabit the bottom, are most sought after and tasty.

Spotted scorpionfish (Scorpaena guttata):

Also called sculpin. Mottled shades of brown and red/orange color. Well camoflaged on the bottom. Sharp poisonous spines. Found shallow to 600 ft deep. Length to 17". Sculpin are very tasty but have sharp venomous spines which makes handling difficult and may be best avoided. If punctured, soak with hot water to relieve pain.

Lingcod (Ophiodon elongatus): Also called lings. Long and somewhat slender body with brown and greenish mottling. Single lateral line. Large mouth with large canine teeth. Fish eggs are poisonous. Weight can reach over 40 lbs (avg 8-12 lbs). Males can be territorial and aggressive. Larger fish prefer deeper waters. Found to 1400 ft deep.

Cabezon (Scorpaenichthys marmoratus): No scales. Length to 39". Found shallow to 250 ft deep. Males guard eggs. Greenish meat turns white when cooked. Lings, cabezon and sculpin may be found camoflaged in crevices or on the bottom. These larger fish hit hard, fight and run into the rocks. Spearfishing and angling is the same as for rockfish. Subdue by thumb and finger in eye sockets.

Fish and game rules for rockfish have many specific variations (depth, season, method etc..) and change often. Check their website for updates.

HALIBUT

California Halibut (Paralichthys californicus):
Also called flatty, fly swatter (small) and
barn door (large). Large flatfish body is
oblong and compressed with a high arched
lateral line over pectoral fin. Head is small with
a very large mouth and numerous sharp teeth. Color is
light to dark gray/brown on the top (eye side) and white on the bottom (blind
side). Length to 60" (72 pounds). Average 5-20 lbs.

Natural history: Halibut begin as small larvae, nourished by a yolk sack. At
2 or 3 days old, juveniles begin swimming, their jaws become functional and
they start feeding. Born with eyes on each side of the head, one eye begins
to migrate over the top of the head and ends up on the same side as the other
eye (usually left). As the eye moves, the larvae begins to swim on its side and
moves toward the bottom (no air bladder). The eyed-side develops a
grayish-brown pigment which can change color to match its surroundings.
Growth rate depends on the habitat. Males mature when 2 or 3 years old, but
females don't mature until 4 or 5 (11-17"). Females grow larger, live longer
(over 30 years), and are more numerous than males. Halibut move into shallow
water to spawn in March through July and feed actively. Mature females can
produce hundreds of thousands of eggs with each spawning (Large 30 to 50
pound females can produce millions). Bays, harbors, and leeward sides of
points and islands can produce warmer water, a more abundant food supply
and create a stable growth environment. In winter, halibut are found in deeper
water (to 600 feet) but most commonly caught in 60 to 120 feet of water. They
are not known to make extensive migrations. From February to July they
move toward shore, just past the surf line (5 to 15 feet), to spawn and feed.
They may stay until early fall. They often move in shallow during a grunion
run. Halibut are found in bays, channels, estuaries, off canyons and long
beaches. They prefer a sandy bottom but can be found on the hard bottoms
(gravel and shale) and muddy bottoms. Large ones can be found in sand
bordered by various structures (rock outcroppings, breakwalls, pilings, wrecks,
moorings, kelp clumps, lobster traps, eel grass beds, sand dollar beds and
clam beds). They're not known to make long migrations. Halibut lay
camouflaged on the bottom and may partially bury themselves in a fine layer
of sand. They're not bottom feeders, they rise off the bottom in an explosive
lunge to grab prey. Halibut feed on anchovies, sardines and small fish (grunion,
smelt, herring, tom cod, small mackerel, small perch, etc.) live or fresh-dead
squid, crustaceans, and mollusks. They've been observed chasing bait fish
near the surface and may jump clear out of the water trying to secure a meal.
Spearfishing is best in the early evening or morning. Halibut can be hunted
by free diving or SCUBA. A pole spear can be used but a small to medium
high powered spear gun is best. A gun with double bands, heavy shaft, rock
point with double wings and a detachable head is very effective. A reel is

helpful for big fish. When hunting, move slowly and quietly as far over the bottom as visibility permits. Be methodical and cover a lot of ground quickly. Drift or glide when possible and keep the spear gun ready. Swimming into the sun gives greater visibility and avoids casting a shadow. Halibut may bury themselves under a thin layer of sand. Look for distinctive halibut shaped outlines or an unusual oval-shaped mound of sand. Search for two eyes staring up. Often, the fins (especially the tail) will remain exposed. A cloud of mud (sand explosion) is usually a sign of a spooked halibut or other bottom dweller. Halibut shaped depressions (prints) may indicate a good area. When halibut are observed or prints occur, concentrate on that area and depth. When sighted, keep the gun aimed at the eyes. Estimate the size of the fish by knowing the length of your spear gun. Slowly move in for the shot. Halibut may rely on camouflage and let a diver pass over, but don't wait too long to shoot. Aim for a spot just behind the gill plate and through the spine. Leave enough distance for the shaft to exit the end of the spear gun. They're a powerful fish, so expect a fight. Use your body weight to pin the fish to the bottom. With fish still on the shaft, reach under the gill plate and rip out the gills to disable the fish. The halibut can now be boated, beached or placed on a stringer (avoid sea lions etc.)

Fishing: Halibut made a came back after gillnets were banned. The season is year-round, but best in the spring. Think about your strategy. Swell plays an important part. A big swell will push the fish into deeper water. If it's rolling, you may be better off drifting bait in 60 feet or more. In good weather, (especially springtime), fish an incoming tide in the afternoon all the way through the outgoing tide. In shallow water the fish become more active as water temperature rises. Some of the best bites are in the last two hours of daylight. The lee sides of major points get the local water warming in the spring, as well as attracting bait fish. A good fish finder helps to determine bait and terrain. Use a 7-8 foot rod, a conventional star-drag reel, 15-30 lb test (clear) main line and a 30 lb leader (prevent breakoffs). Presentation of the bait is the key. Big baits for big fish! Top halibut baits include mackerel (heads or guts), anchovies, sardines, herring, cod, crab, squid, queenfish, white croakers, shiner perch and halibut skin (white side). Using a drift rig (pg 100) to drift live bait on sandy flats is the best fishing method. Cast out, when you feel the bait hit the bottom, take up the slack. Back drag off just enough so they can not take line out. Keep the rod steady and use just the reel to bounce the bait off the bottom (about 3 cranks). Stop, wait until you hit bottom again, and repeat. Change bait every 15 to 30-minutes. Rake-marks on the bait means fish are in the area. Halibut are relatively aggressive fish. Watch the rod tip and wait for a sharp tap. When bit, wind in steady until you feel the fish loaded up on the rod, then swing the rod to set the hook. Halibut need to be played with firm steady pressure (not aggressive pumping). Use rod tip to absorb the wicked halibut head shakes. When boated, they need to be handled gently. Don't put your hands in their gills or squeeze them too hard. Using a fine mesh net will allow you to catch and release the fish without any damage.

SANDDAB

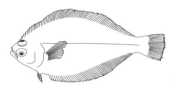

Pacific sanddab (Citharichthys sordidus): Member of the Bothidae family (left-eyed flounders). Also called soft flounder, mottled sanddab and sole. Body is oblonged and compressed. Light brown mottled with yellow and orange on the eye side (top) and white on bottom. Can change color and pattern to match surroundings. Latteral line is nearly straight. Pectoral fin is shorter than the head. Pacific sanddab is always has eyes on left side. Length to 16" (11.5" is just over 1/2 lb). They live on deep sandy bottoms. Found 30 to 1800 ft deep, they are most abundant at depths of 120 to 300 feet. Spawning peaks form July through September and probably spawn more than once each season. Females lay numerous eggs. They live on sandy bottoms. Main diet is small fish, squid, octopus, various eggs, sea squirts, shrimp, crabs and marine worms.

Longfin sanddab (Citharichthys xanthostigma): Similar to pacific sanddab. Uniform dark brown color with orange and white speckles on the top (eye side) and the blind side (bottom) is white. Head is deep and eyes are large. Pectoral fin is longer than head, compared to Pacific sanddab which is shorter than head. Length to 15.5 inches.

Fishing: Few fishermen concentrate on sanddabs, probably because of their small size and depth. Other small flounders (pg 105) are usually caught incidentally. Some consider sanddabs the best tasting of all ocean fish. Sanddabs are caught commercially, and served in many fine restaurants. Sanddabs are plentiful in coastal bays and when ocean waters are warmer than usual. They are voracious feeders. A good bottom and proper depth should produce fish. Most are caught from 120-300 feet deep. A sensitive-tipped rod, to feel the bites, with a 6/0 rockcod reel works fine. Rig similar to a rock cod gangnion (pg 101) with several small hooks on a line. There are currently no restrictions on number of hooks used (7-8 is popular). Some use a ring device, with many baited hooks, on a heavy rock cod rod. The ring is set just off the botton with hooks dangling. This rig keeps hooks from tangling and is baited less often. Use cut pieces (strips) of squid, pile worms, grass shrimp or ghost shrimp for bait. Squid works best because it's tough and stays on the hook. Double hooking helps keep the bait on. Best if no swells or currents. Occasionally fish (schools of mackerel) will hit the bait on the way down. Keep the rig on the bottom since this is where the flatfish feed. Sand dabs bite in flurries or waves. Learn to feel the subtle strikes. With each hit, set the hook. When the bites stop (possibly some twitching), either each hook has a sanddab or the bait is gone. Feel the weight of the line get heavier with fish then reel in steadily. Dropping down, reeling up, removing caught fish and re-baiting hooks takes time so make the most out of every cast.

SHEEPHEAD

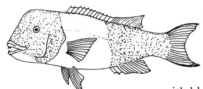

Sheephead (Semicossyphus pulcher): are born as females (dull pink with white chin). After about 5 years (12"), they change (hermaphodite) into males. Males have black head with blunt forehead, large protruding buck teeth and white chin. Middle of thick body is red and tail is black. Length to 36" (36 lbs).

Natural history: Sheephead spawn in early spring and summer. Juvenile sheephead (1/2") are bright red/orange with 2 black spots on dorsal fin and one on tail. They appear from May-Dec, staying close to the rocks. At 6 years they take on the female color. They have powerful jaws and a special plate in their throat to crush shells. They inhabit nearshore rocky kelp areas to 180' deep (usually 20-120 ft). They feed on urchins, sea cucumbers, squid, snails, clams and mussels.

Spearfishing: Sheephead can get very large but the best eating size is about 14 to 18 inches. Shooting distance is less than open ocean so equipment suited to kelp and rock is helpful. A pole spear with multi-tined or paralyzer tip can be used for small fish. Most hunters prefer a short to medium-sized speargun. Thick rock pointed tips with double wings and a spinner head to prevent the fish from twisting off is effective. SCUBA divers may wish to adapt the gun to negative buoyancy so it can be set down on the bottom. Carrying a small light can be useful in caves and crevices. Stalk or float quietly in the open channels of the kelp bed waiting for fish to swim by. Use rocks and kelp for cover during descent or while hunting. Move slowly and quietly with gun extended and ready. Try getting under the fish and shooting up. Aim at a spot behind the gill plate and into the spine. Large sheephead have thick scales and are best shot from behind. Search the bottom, caves and crevasses for rockfish. Spotting fish takes time and patience. Line up the shot to avoid direct impact with rocks. Allow enough distance for the spear shaft to exit the end of the speargun. Use caution when diving in kelp, know the location of other divers, to avoid accidents. Once speared, place small fish in a game bag or on a stringer before removing from the shaft. Stringers may be attached to the diver using a quick release or to a surface float. Larger fish should be beached or boated.

Fishing: Live fish trapping of sheephead targeting 1-4 lb females has diminished sheephead populations. New regulations on trapping and fishing have been issued. Sheephead are fished on or near the bottom using squid, anchovy or whole mackerel (large fish). Prepare for a battle as fish will use kelp and rocks to escape. **Check F & G rules for updates.**

KELP (CALICO) BASS

Kelp (Calico) Bass (Paralabrax clathratus): Body is elongate and compressed. Color is camoflaged brownish olive/green with light yellowish blotches on back becoming lighter below. Head has a relatively pointed snout and large mouth. Length to 28" (18 lbs).

Natural History: The spawning season usually extends from May through September, peaking in July. By the time kelp bass are 5 years old (11-12 in) nearly all are capable of spawning. Growth is slow, a 9 year old is about 16.5 inches and it takes 20 years to reach 23 inches (5 lbs). Calico's inhabit the kelp beds and nearshore reefs staying a few feet below the surface to the mid water depths. They hang in the eddies behind rocks that block currents and wait in ambush for an unsuspecting prey to happen by. They feed on small shrimp-like crustaceans, anchovies, small surfperch, and other small fishes. Calico's may move deeper (to 150 ft) in winter or hide in structures (wrecks, moorings). They do not migrate.

Spearfishing: They may rest in rock crevices or be found swimming in and around kelp. Similar to sheephead spearfishing (pg 129). They are a cunning, "streetwise" fish that spook easily. Often you spot each other at the same time. Line up and shoot quickly. Forget trying to chase them!

Fishing: In addition to kelp beds, Calico are found around seawalls, shallow water reefs, boilers, near lobster traps and other structures. They're voracious feeders and even small bass will hit large baits. Use a strong 7.5-8 foot rod and conventional reel (tight drag) with 15-20 lb test line. Skill is required to hook and land them consistently. Most common technique is fly lining (pg 100) a live bait (anchovies, sardines, brown herring, and squid), hooked to swim easily. Toss into the edge of kelp beds allowing bait to take line freely. Use a small weight to get bait down into structures and to help contol the bait. Calico readily take artificial lures (cast plugs, spoons, candy bars and jigs), especially in green and brown water. Good colors are a yellow, bronze, or white colored jig. Lead headed (with eye), single tailed, plastic swim baits, work very well. Popular colors are greens, browns and reds . Darker colors in gray light and lighter colors by day. Effectiveness may be improved by adding of a long thin strip of squid to the hook of the lure. A thin strip doesn't restrict the normal action of the lure. Imitate a nervous bait fish with slow twitchy movements. Try throwing into a structure and then drag over it. Keep the rod tip up, reel in gear and be ready. Slow trolling a short line (15-20 ft) with swimming plugs (Rapalas etc.), close as possible to rocks and underwater structures. Calico are noted for their fighting qualities. When hooked, pull the fish away from kelp or structure quickly. If they turn and run, it's more dificult to turn them back. Don't spend a lot time in a spot with no strikes.

BARRACUDA

California Barracuda (Sphyraena argentea): Also called cuda, scooter and barries. Silvery colored body is long and slender with wide spaced dorsal fins and yellow tail. Head is sharp pointed with protruding jaw. Mouth is large with numerous sharp canine like teeth. Length to 48" (20 lbs) usually less than 36".

Natural History: The banning of gill nets and the current 28" minimum size limit has allowed most all barracuda to breed. In the early spring (Feb-Apr), they move up from deep water into the near shore areas to spawn. Spawning season is April through September (mostly May - July). Juvinile (6 ") barracuda are found in shallow water. Barrauda range from the surface to deep water moving quickly over a wide range. In summer they cruise the edge of the kelp beds searching for small bait fish and may chase schools of bait through the inshore flats. Usually, this coastal school fish will work as a tight group or may spread out over several miles. Barracuda are harmless in the water. They only strike at what they can eat whole.

Fishing: Season is year round but best from May through October. Look for birds working bait on the surface or jumping out of the water. Lighter outfits with 15 lb mono line works. Barracuda are easily caught on lures (feathers, spoons, bone jigs, flies, plastic swim baits and plugs) or bait. Match the size (3-5") and color of lure to the natural baitfish. Flashy chrome, white, blue/white (anchovy) and green/white (sardine) colors work best. Try shiny chrome jigs at night. For deeper fish, try a chrome sinker attached above the leader. Single hook jigs are preferred. Treble hooks are harder to remove and will damage the fish's mouth. Releasing a fish with a damaged mouth often causes death. Cast out as far as possible and let the lure sink in the water column for a few seconds. Retrieve at a medium speed, fast enough for the lure action. Also try pumping the lure. Lures can also be trolled about 40 to 50 feet behind boat at 3 to 5 knots (or whatever works the lure). Prepare to go through lots of the more fragile lures (plugs, flies and swim baits). Barracuda also will take live anchovies or sardines fly lined near the kelp or dropped down with a small rubber core, sliding sinker or split shot. These fish hit hard and are used to killing their prey instantly with their crushing jaws. Their long narrow mouth and slashing strikes make it harder to set the hook. You may get several hits per retrieve before a hooking up. Once hooked, slowly reel in with constant pressure. Jerking the fish in allows their sharp teeth to cut through a mono leader. Before casting out again, check your leader for nicks and other damage. Using short wire leaders will result in less strikes and fewer losses. They are strong vigorous fighters, making hard turns, shaking their heads and are fun to catch. Use caution when handling a landed fish. They are strong, have numerous sharp teeth and will thrash about on deck. Grab barracuda just behind the head, then slip your fingers under the gill plates and hold the neck. They can be pretty slimy and hard to hold. Put on ice ASAP.

YELLOWTAIL & DORADO

Yellowtail (Seriola lalandi): Member of the Jack family. Also called amberjack, forktail and kingfish. The head is conical with a sharp snout. Long silvery blue/green body with dark horizontal yellow stripe from eye to tail. Yellow/green tail is slender and deep forked. Length to 60" (80 lbs). Few over 40 lbs (average 15 lbs).

Natural History: Spawning occurs from June through October. Yellowtail grow quickly are sexually mature in two years and all will spawn by three years old. A three year old female (10 lbs) spawns about 450,000 eggs and a 25 pounder spawns over 1 million eggs. Lifespan is 10-12 yrs. Yellowtail are fast, aggressive, opportunistic feeders (usually daytime) eating anything that is abundant in the area including red crabs, anchovies, squid, and most small fishes. Herding schools of bait into tight balls, they attack with intense ferocity, gorging themselves . When the water temperature rises above 62°F (early spring) they migtate from Mexico in search of schools of squid. These pelagic schooling fish are found near kelp beds of offshore islands, along ridges, over seamounts and under kelp paddies. They stay close to deep water but are usually found in the warmer areas (surface to 30 ft deep). Depths range from surface to 228 ft. By October, they return south for the winter. However, some stragglers spend the entire year in California.

Spearfishing: Hunting is best from May to July (continues through Oct) when fish move into warmer water. Free diving is the best way to hunt (pg 90), but SCUBA divers can be successful. Use a large blue water gun with detachable tip and float or reel. Early morning (red sky is best) and early evening are good times to hunt. Search the up current, outside edges and channels of kelp beds, pinnacles and the seaward side of rocky points. Kelp paddies (especially big ones) draw bait fish and yellowtail. Yellowtail are difficult to spot, approach and shoot. A colony defense enables a single fish to quickly warn all others. To hunt, drop down 20-30 ft, then hang and observe. Some yellowtail are wary of divers while others are curious and may be attracted by several methods. Slapping your hand on the water to immitate bait fish feeding. Waving a white glove or removing a glove and wiggling fingers. Strumming the rubber bands of your gun or tapping your gun on the weight belt. Schooling fish are usually easier to approach. Bigger fish tend to be solitary or with a few others. When lining up the shot, swim with the fish, not at it. Yellowtail are a powerfull and aggressive fish, capable of pulling you under, so expect a fight.

Fishing: With warmer waters and the ban on gill nets, yellowtail have made comeback. Yellowtail are often found under and around (to 30 yds) kelp beds and floating paddies. Usually found in 66-70°F water. A 7-8 ft rod, conventional reel and 15-30 lb mono line works. Set drag to about 1/3 of line breaking strength. Get out at early morning first or sunset (at gray light). Search the ocean surface for birds working bait, kelp paddies, something on the fish finder, boil action and other fishermen. Slow troll (40 yds behind boat) past kelp beds or paddies, check the meter and look for fish (polarized sungalsses help). Start up wind or current, turn off engine and drift by. Approach slowly, quiet and not too close to the paddie. Toss in a few anchovies and see if fish attack. Cast beyond the kelp (not in front) so you don't get tangled. Live squid, fly lined with a 3/0 live bait hook is the best method. Allow the bait to run for a few minutes. If live squid is not available then a green backed sardine (nose hooked with a 1/0 hook) anchovy, smelt, mackerel (neck hooked) or fresh dead squid. For deeper fish use a 1-6 oz sliding egg sinker allow the bait to sink (up to 100 ft). Yellowtail will take most any type of lure (jigs, feathers, plugs and rubber swim baits). Use dark colors early in the morning and late afternoon and brighter colors during the day. To fish iron's, throw a light (up to 3 oz) iron close to the paddie, count to10 and retrieve with a jigging motion. Be prepared for the fish to hit it on the way down. When you feel a strike, count to 3 and set the hook. If you miss the fish, reel the bait in slowly, the fish may strike again. You can also anchor where yellowtail frequent and chum with live anchovies. In spring, try fishing the bottom. A bottom fishing outfit with dropper loop rig (pg 101), baited with live squid or mackerel (neck hooked). Big bait for big fish. The strike may be vicious followed by long deep runs and a fierce battle until the fish is exhausted. They often head for obstacles (kelp, rocks or anchor line) so set drag to heavy, pull hard quickly and try to get them to the boat as fast as possible.

Dorado (Coryphaena hippurus): Also called dolphin fish and mahi mahi. A blaze of blue and yellow or deep green and yellow when in the water. Small dark spots on sides. Dorsal fin extends nearly from head to tail.

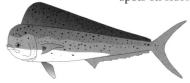

Head is blunt in males (bulls) and rounded in females (cows). Weight to 87 lbs. (avg. 10 to 30 lbs).

Natural history: Dorado are seasonal, blue water fish, moving up from Mexico with warm currents. Usually located near kelp paddies or floating debris. Dolphin roam the open sea in a continuous hunt for food. Schooling fish run in similar sizes. Larger fish are either loners or a paired bull and cow. Males can exceed 80 lbs and females about 40 lbs.

Fishing: Techniques are the same as for yellowtail. Season is Aug - Nov (best Sep-Oct) when water reaches 72° F +. A school of dorado may be kept around the boat by chumming with cut bait and or by keeping a hooked fish in the water. If strikes slow down, cut bait often does the trick. Large or wise fish may only hit live baits. When hooked or excited, it rapidly changes colors and sometimes shows dark vertical stripes. Dorado are great fighters, fast (to 50 MPH), strong and acrobatic (great jumpers).

WHITE SEABASS

White seabass (Atractoscion nobilis): Not true "seabass" but croakers. Lower jaw extends past upper jaw. Juveniles have several dark vertical bars. Length to 60 in / 83 lbs.

Natural history: In March, these pelagic (open ocean) predators migrate to the island to spawn in the inshore kelp beds. Seabass spawn through August peaking in May and June. Mature white seabass group close to shore over rocky habitat usually near kelp beds during the spawning season. Females probably spawn hundreds of thousands to millions of eggs depending on the size of the fish. Larval seabass develop in the plankton for about 5 wks (1/4 in) then settle to the bottom just outside the surf zone (in drift algae) along open coast sandy beaches. They remain in this nursery habitat for about a year (10 in). Yearlings then begin to move around and can be found with older juveniles in shallow, nearshore habitats (reefs, kelp beds, harbors and bays). After 4 yrs (24 in), about 50% of male white seabass are mature. About 50% of females are mature and can lay eggs at 5 yrs (28 in). They move deeper (to 350 ft) in winter feeding on squid, anchovies, sardines, pelagic red crabs, and other small fish. They probably live to 20 yrs.

Spearfishing: Seabass are the greatest challenge for Catalina hunters. is best from May to July when fish move into shallow water to breed. Early morning and early evening is a good time to hunt. They are wary and easily alerted by SCUBA bubbles. Free diving is the best method of hunting. Seabass demand the biggest gun you can load with either a float or reel to fight them (pg 90). This is the hardest and most prized fish to hunt and will require a lot of learning, practice and experience before you see or shoot a fish. You need to be quiet, blend in to the background and be aware. Knowlege of tidal changes, currents and their relation to the fish is important. Early morning and early evening is best. Listen carefully for their deep croaking sound, watch bait fish for reactions and observe seabirds diving as indications of possible fish. In good visibility, hunt from the surface. In less visibility, drop down 20-30 ft and hunt up (sillouettes). Search the up current, outside edges and channels of kelp beds, kelp paddies, reefs, pinnacles and rocky points. In early morning you may find a sleeper (10-40 ft deep) in the kelp. They're difficult to spot, approach and can appear quickly, so be ready to shoot. The slightest movement or noise can spook the fish, causing it to instantly disappear. A colony defense system enables a single fish to quickly warn all others. Seabass may be curious and occasionally attracted. Innovative techniques include imitating their croaking sound to call them, strumming the rubber gun bands like guitar strings or waving a white glove. Only take a good shot. Aim for the head where the lateral line meets the gill plate. These are powerful fish so expect a fight. Once hit, quickly dive down to the the fish and try to subdue it before it has time to recover.

Fishing: White seabass is the premiere game fish of Catalina anglers. They are making comeback after the ban on gill netting. Most anglers start looking for seabass around March but the best months are April through June when the squid are mating. Seabass are a near shore fish, usually traveling in schools over rocky bottoms and around kelp beds. Fishing near the bottom in a sandy area is usually best. Seabass fishing is usually a drop down and wait type of fishing. A 7-8 ft rod and conventional reel with 25-30 lb test line should work fine. Flylining a live squid is the best, but anchovies, sardines and blacksmith are also effective. Match the hook to the size of your bait, but most fishing is done with a 3/0-4/0 live bait hook. A sliding egg sinker or rubber core is added just ahead of the hook to help take the bait down. Once rigged, hook up a lively bait and drop it to the bottom. A combination of white candy bar, with trebble hook, baited with 2 to 3 live squid is very effective. This rig may simulate squid mating. They will hit bare lures, worked vertically, but not often. If you are anchored up on a good seabass hole with a good current running, rig up a second rod with lever drag reel and a dropper loop rig with a squid on each hook. Whatever rig you use, drop it down to the bottom then reel up several feet (6-10 turns) above the bottom. Set the rod in a holder and let the movement of the boat work the bait. Keep the reel out of gear with the clicker on. Set the drag heavy enough to set the hooks but not so much as to jerk the rod out of the holder. If the fish hits hard, too much drag could even break the rod. Seabass may hit with a soft nibble or extremely hard and can quickly run line off the reel. They tend to fight a hard, tenacious battle for a few minutes and then give up considerably and can be reeled right in. They often try to use the kelp and other structures to get tangled and escape. The Hubbs-Sea World Research Institute hatchery at Carlsbad supplies the Catalina Seabass Fund with small (4 in) white seabass. Two grow-out pens in Cat Harbor are used to raise the seabass to larger fish. Over 80,000 juveniles have been released in island waters. Most released fish tend to stay in protected waters for about a year and then move to outside waters. Many small hatchery fish inhabit West Cove (Cactus Bay). Hatchery seabass are tagged by inserting a 1/8" stainless steel wire in the cheek of the fish. The tagged fish are now reaching legal size. Hubbs is requesting anglers to remove the head and send it to the hatchery to be checked for a tag. Please attach a tag indicating when and where the fish was caught, length and weight. The information is invaluable for research. Some anglers remove the ear stones (two small calcium growths) from the ear canals within the heads. Ear stones are collected by some as trophies or they can be made into jewelry. Removing the stones will not affect the checking of the tags. Locations accepting seabass heads are posted on the hatchery website at www.hswri.org. Two Harbors sponsors the Catalina Seabass tournament each May which is also used to collect heads for research.

TUNAS

Some tuna (also called ahi) are regular visitors to Southern California and others may only arrive occasionally. Water temperature is important and various species arrive as water temperatures rise. The most targeted gamefish is albacore. Bigeye, bluefin and yellowfin are sometimes caught incidentally and bonito, though fun to catch, are marginal as gamefish. These are blue water fish and the most productive areas are often the offshore banks (pg 80) or sub-sea mountain ranges.

Albacore (Thunnus alalunga): Also called longfin and albie. Body is cigar-shaped and tapered at both ends. Head is long with fairly large mouth. Color is dark gray to metallic blue on the back becoming white to gray below. Extremely long pectoral fins (extend well past anal fin). Length to 60 in / 79 lbs (avg 25-50 lbs).

Natural History: Albacore spawning probably occurs NW of Hawaii. Like most tunas, they're opportunistic feeders taking what's most available in the area (small fishes, squid, octopus and crustaceans). Albacore travel in very fast, loose schools. Albacore migrate almost 5,000 miles annualy from California to Japan in just 294 days (over 17 miles a day).

Fishing for albacore is Mar-Nov (best May-Jul) in 63-67° F water. A sea water temperature gauge will help put you on spots. They're rarely taken near shore (usually 20-100 miles offshore). Offshore banks are productive areas and keep an eye out for kelp paddies, feeding birds, whales and porpoises. Jigs are used to locate the schools, then live anchovies are chummed to keep the fish around the boat. Use a trolling rig with a 6-8 foot leader and 30-50 lb test. Deciding which jig to use (mini feathers, tuna clones, etc...) is important. Check what the tuna are feeding on and match the jig to the bait fish (easier after dark with deck lights). Try a favorite jig that has worked in the past or just experiment and prepare to switch jigs until you find what works. Jig hooks can be either single or double. Troll jigs behind the boat at a moderate speed (6-8 knots). Every boat has a different wake, so find a pattern that puts your jigs in clean water where albacore can see them and where the jig swims best. Try a W pattern (pg 138) with inside jigs on the second or third wake back, and the outside jigs on the third and fourth. Set less than 100 feet out to draw fish to the boat easier. Troll a bit faster when scouting for signs of fish or running. Adding a whiskey line (down the middle) may increase the number of hook ups. If marking fish deep on the meter, try figure eight turns while slowly chumming pieces of cut bait. This creates a "ladder" or trail of bait for the fish to follow to the surface. After a jig strike, keep the boat going a short distance to increase chance of multiple hook ups. Match the fishing gear to the fish and bait. Too light will cause long battles and too heavy may cause bad presentation. Tuna in a feeding frenzy will hit almost any silvery object. Once stopped, toss live bait on the surface to attract the feeding fish. Flyline a lively bait (anchovy or sardine) and avoid slack in the line. Big hooks and heavy lines make it difficult to keep bait lively so use as light a line as posible. Size the hooks to the line (2/0 hook for 20 lb line, 3/0 for 30 lb, 4/0 for 40 lb etc...). Leaving a hooked fish in the water may hold a school near. Once hooked, expect a powerful fight. They have great determination and endurance. Follow the fish with the rod and let the drag tire the fish. Once fish is boated, check its stomach contents to determine diet. Bleed and put on ice ASAP.

Bigeye tuna (Thunnus obesus): Body is cigar-shaped (tapered at both ends). Head is pointed and the eye is relatively large. Color is dark metallic brownish blue to dark yellow on the back becoming gray or whitish below. There often is a bluish stripe on the side. Pectoral fins which extend well past anal fin.

Natural History: Diet includes fishes, squid, and crustaceans. Apr-Sep, bigeye (3 yrs/45 lbs) start spawning, near the equatorial Pacific. A 159 lb bigeye produces over 3 million eggs per year. They live 7 or 8 years.

Fishing season for bigeye is late Jun (65°F) - Nov. Sep - Oct is best in water over 70°F (best 72°F+). They're usually found below the surface, occasionaly comming up to feed. Because they're hard to locate, most bigeye are taken incidentally when albacore or marlin fishing.

Bluefin Tuna (Thunnus thynnus): Also called leaping tuna, footballs, tunny, shortfin tuna and great albacore. Body is cigar-shaped and thick with a fairly large mouth. Color is dark blue above and gray below. Relatively short pectoral fins. Weight to 363 lbs (avg is 1-2 yrs old / 15-30 lbs).

Natural history: Bluefin diet is mostly anchovies, but sanddabs, surfperches, and white croakers are also consumed.

Fishing: Bluefin occasionally appear from May-Oct (best May-July) in water temperatures from 63°- 68° F. They can be located by either trolling feathers or anchoring at a spot known to be frequented by bluefin tuna, and chumming with live anchovies. Once the fish are attracted, anglers must use light line (12# test or less), small hooks (#4's or smaller), and the "hottest" bait available that season (usually live anchovies or pieces of squid).

Yellowfin tuna (Thunnus albacares): Also called Pacific yellowfin. Body is cigar-shaped and head is conical. Color is dark brownish blue to dark yellow on the back becoming whitish gray below. Pectoral fins do not extend past the anal fin. Larger fish may have an elongated second dorsal fin. Length to 80 in / 435 lbs (avg 50-100 lbs). Largest yellowfin are over 10 years old.

Natural History: Yellowfin tuna spawn in the eastern Pacific. Some spawning takes place year round. Juveniles grow rapidly and weigh about 7.5 lbs at 1.5 years and 150 lbs at 4 years. Diet includes small fish, crustaceans, and squid.

Fishing season for yellowfin is Aug-Nov (best Sept-Oct) in water temperature over 70° F (best over 74° F). Yellowfin are fished same as albacore. Most yellowfin tuna taken in California weigh 30 to 50 pounds, fish over 200 pounds are occasionally landed. The smaller fish are 1 to 2 years.

MAKO SHARK

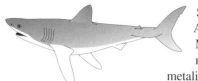

Shortfin Mako Shark: (Isurus oxyrinchus). Also called bonito, mako or mackerel shark. Makos have long gill slits. The body of the mako is elongate, stout and colored deep metalic blue to dark gray above with white below. The head is long and conical with pointed snout (dark on top) and a mouth full of razor sharp teeth, visibly protruding on lower jaw. Length to 13 ft / 1,000 lbs (average 10 ft / 300 lbs).

Natural History: The Southern California Bight (indentation along the Southern California coast) is a nursery ground for newborn and juvenile sharks. Mako's are sexually mature at 4-6 years. Mako's and threshers do not reproduce in large numbers. Mako's have a 15 to 18 month gestation and may bear several more live pups (29" / 13 lbs) which can be cannibalistic in utero. Juvenile mako's (2-3 yrs old / 59 in / 99 lbs), spend most of their time within 40 feet of the surface, while older sharks spend more time at greater depths. Mako's feed mainly on bony fishes such as sardines, mackerels, bonitos, tunas and squid. Marine mammals are rarely eaten. Mako's will also chase down swordfish and bite off the tail to incapacitate them. They often bear scars from these encounters. Whenever possible, the Mako takes food in one gulp. Like tunas, makos maintain body temperatures, in their muscles, above ambient water temperatures. This enhances muscle power and efficiency while swimming. The mako is the fastest shark, propelling themselves through the water with short strokes of their thick, powerful tails, at over 20 MPH and may travel 36 miles per day. The mako shark is sleek, muscular and spectacularly acrobatic. Makos do not school, are usually solitary and seldom seen together in large numbers.

Fishing Information: Fishing begins in early spring and is best during the summer months. Mako's are more abundant than threshers. Perfered temperature for makos is 59-63° F. The tackle used has to be heavy. A popular outfit is a heavy conventional 2 speed reel with 80 pound dacron line on a stiff 6 ft. rod with all roller guides and a gimbled butt. Basic rig is a 9/0 to 12/0 hook attached to a 10' heavy wire leader. The best ways to hook a mako is by trolling or drifting through a chum slick. slow troll a whole bonito, mackerel (best), squid or a combination of lure and bait. A downrigger can be used to fish in lower depths. The prefered method is to release a chum "slick" of ground fish and small pieces of bait. Into this slick, whole dead mackerel are floated below bobbers made of either a rubber balloon or a plastic water bottle. Shark fishing takes skill and teamwork. A three man crew works best. The skipper keeps the boat in gear most of the time to keep the action straight back. The Angler fights the fish. The third person has to clear the decks of all other lines and down riggers, relieves the angler, and gaffs the keepers with a flying gaff. When hooked, they often put on an aerial demonstration (Mako's can jump 20 feet high) or require a brute strength battle beneath the surface. Watch out, when you catch one, Makos will use their sharp teeth to attack you or your boat.

THRESHER SHARK

Common Thresher Shark: (Alopias vulpinus). Also called thresher, blue thresher, green thresher, longtail shark or swiveltail. Distinctive long tail (almost as long as it's body). The thresher has tiny teeth and small mouth relative to it's size. Color may vary from brownish gray, bluish or blackish above to silvery, bluish or golden below. The dorsal, pectoral and ventral fins are blackish. Pectoral and ventral fins may have a white dot in the tip. The bigeye thresher, also found off the California coast, can be distinguished by its large eye and fewer teeth. Length to 20 feet and weighing 1,000 pounds (15' is common).

Natural History: Thresher's become sexually mature in 6 to 7 years and females bear about 4 live pups annually. Thresher's and mako's are two of the larger sharks in California waters and females grow larger than males. While primarily pelagic, they may be also found inshore. The common thresher is found of the upper layers of deep offshore waters and is most abundant along the edges (steep bottom drop off) of the continental shelf. They occur worldwide in warmer seas. Diet is mainly sardines, mackerel, anchovies and squid (often large ones). They use their long tail to flail, frighten, stun prey and as a potent weapon. During the spring and summer months smaller threshers may occur near shore where they are often seen leaping completely out of the water. An 18 foot thresher female contained four young, each weighing 13.5 pounds and were 4 to 4.5 feet long.

Fishing Information: Most thresher sharks are taken by slow trolling live sardines, anchovies, or mackerel. The basic outfit and rig is same as for mako. For threshers, downriggers, using 15 pound down rigger balls (reflective tape removed to prevent attacks), are productive. Dual down riggers, one deep and the other one half way up, will cover the entire water column. Good quality sharks are found around 80 feet down. Find some bait on the meter then slow troll (about 3 knots) a wired mackerel. Put teasers on the outriggers and stay alert. When hooked, they may jump or require a brute strength battle beneath the surface. Threshers pull hard, using their tail to make long runs. These are large, tough fish so expect a long fight. Watch out, when you catch one, a threasher's tail is rummored to have decapitated a fisherman.

Many biologists are concerned that continued over fishing might cause the shark population to crash. Makos are a secondary target of the swordfish and thresher commercial fisheries. Gillnetting decimated the, once numerous, blue sharks in the San Pedro Channel. Although larger mako sharks have commercial value, many small makos and blue sharks have little commercial value and are discarded as bycatch. Removing large numbers of young sharks is a serious detriment to the future population. We could be moving toward a time when sharks become rare. Practice catch and release.

MARLIN & SWORDFISH

Striped Marlin (Tetrapturus audax): Member of the billfish family. Also called stripes, striper, pacific marlin and spikefish. Smaller than the blue marlin.

Body is elongate and compressed with fins on the belly. Color is dark cobalt electric blue that fades to a silvery white underside. Named for the light blue/lavender vertical stripes (14 to 20) or spots on the sides. Marlin scales are covered with a layer of heavy skin so they are not easily seen. Upper jaw extends, forming a long rounded spear. Dorsal fin is light purplish/violet blue with many dark spots. The anterior part of the dorsal and second dorsal are pointed. Pointed pectoral fins can fold against the body. Length to 13.5 feet / 339 pounds (avg 100-175 lbs).

Natural History: Striped marlin are believed to spawn in the Northwest Pacific and migrate eastward as juveniles, accounting for numerous small fish in Hawaiian waters. Tagged fish have migrated 3,120 miles and traveled up to 31 miles per day (farthest of any billfish). Marlin can't be accurately aged, but females probably reach first maturity at 50-80 lb. They are usually solitary until mating. The food of striped marlin is mostly fishes, with some squid, crabs and shrimp. The spear of the marlin can be used as a weapon or to help capture food. Wood hull boats have been rammed by billfish and in one instance the spear penetrated 18.5 inches of hardwood. When using its bill in capturing food, the striped marlin may stun its prey by slashing the bill sideways rather than spearing its victim.

Fishing: Season begins in late July (70°F+) and runs into November. (best Sep-Oct / 72°F+). Fishing is best in deep blue water (over banks pg 80) in an area from the east end of Santa Catalina Island offshore to San Clemente Island and south to the Los Coronados Islands. Most striped marlin are taken by trolling artificial lures or casting bait. A basic rig uses a 4/0 class reel with 300 to 500 yards of 30-50 lb line on a 30-50 lb rod with roller guides and tip. Bright colored (psychedelic) marlin jigs are trolled in areas where marlin are suspected to be, waiting for a fish to strike. Marlin jigs (1 or 2 hooks) come in great variety (names like Kona Clone, Mean Joe Green etc) and cost $20 to $60 and up. Try darker

4 lures in W formation

colored jigs in the morning and brighter colors during the day. Be prepared to change and experiment with differnt lures. Keep hooks honed and sharp. Pictured is a four lure spread in a **W** formation. Generally, troll the 2 short flat lines between the 2nd and 3rd wake and 2 longer outrigger lines on the

4th and 5th wake at 6.5 to 9 knots. Every boat's wake is different and trolling pattern (staggered or pairs), boat speed and jig action will vary. Try to keep the jigs in clear blue water. Boats equiped with extended outriggers can troll jigs outside the wake with a wider pattern. While trolling, keep an eye out (sight fishing) and scope (binoculars) for birds working and marlin swimming on the surface. Marlin thrashing on the surface (feeder) is worth trolling by or casting a bait. Marlin laying motionless on the surface (sleeper) may be approached and bait casted toward the head. Tails sticking up in the air (tailers) can be waited for down swell, then put a bait in front of and past the fish and reel back towards it. Marlin putting on an aerial show (jumpers) are fun to watch but usually not in a feeding mode. They may hit a lure trolled past the fish. Have a mackerel (prefered bait) hooked through the nose ready in the bait tank. If a fish is sighted and showing interest, cast a bait directly astern then slow boat to under 2 knots. Strikes usually result from properly presented live bait. Stripers can "light up" to a brilliant lavender to purple with an intensity not found in other marlin. This is a large powerful fish so prepare for a battle. Don't be surprised if a tuna, dorado, mako or thresher shark hits the jig or bait. Billfish populations are declining, so practice catch and release.

Swordfish (Xiphias gladius): Also called broadbill. Body is elongate and somewhat compressed. Upper jaw is extended, forming a long, flat sword (bill). Swordfish have no scales or ventral fins (fins on the belly) and only

one keel (small projection) on the base of the tail adjoining the fish. Color is deep purple to dark gray above becoming gray to yellowish below. Length to 15 feet / 503 lbs (avg 100-300 lbs).

Natural History: The diet of swordfish includes fishes such as anchovies, hake, jack mackerel, rockfishes, lanternfishes, pencil smelt, as well as squid (giant). Swordfish do not spawn off the coast of California, but in 1958 a female (containing an estimated 50 million eggs) was harpooned off Santa Catalina Island. Spawning peaks is in June and July, but females may lay eggs every month of the year. Eggs take 2.5 days to hatch. They probably grow quite rapidly and do not live very long.

Fishing: Swordfish are taken from May through November, and occasionally landed in December. Usually found between the mainland and the Channel Islands. Few people go out specifically angling for swordfish (occasionally when marlin fishing) and usually less than 20 are caught per year. Fishing basically involves seeing a fish that is finning or sunning on the surface and then working a baited hook in front of it. Live pacific mackerel or dead squid (giant works well) are the preferred baits. Live barracuda can also be used. Once hooked, swordfish are strong, powerful fighters and battles may last over 4 hours. Some fish are landed quickly as fish may swim within gaffing distance of the boat early in the battle.

FISH CLEANING

(Keep fish fresh. Gut and put on ice ASAP)

Filleting
(most popular method of cutting away the flesh from bones and skin)

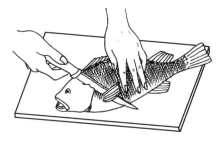

Use a good quality, long thin, sharp knife. Place cold fish on a smooth cutting board. Make the first cut just behind the gill plate (dorsal fin to the pelvic fin) and slice down diagonally toward the head. Cut to the backbone, but not through it or into the guts.

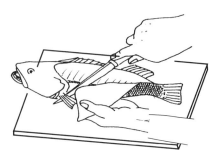

Make a shallow cut (to the backbone), along the dorsal fin from head to tail. Turn the blade and slide it along the backbone and dorsal fin toward the tail while pulling the meat away from the fish. Turn the fish over and repeat on the other side. The fillets are removed leaving the remainder of fish and guts intact. On larger fish the cheeks are also worth saving

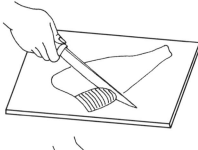

Slide the knife along the rib bones and remove the rib section from both fillets.

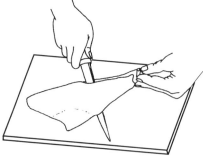

To remove the skin, place fillet on a cutting board, skin side down and cut a 1/2 inch wedge at the tail for a finger grip (to hold skin). Keep the knife at an angle (pressing into the board) and shave the meat from the skin using a gentle sawing action. Boneless and skinless fillets are lightly rinsed ready to cook.

Dressing

Make the first cut just behind the gills and slice down diagonally toward the head. Cut to the bone. Cut belly from tail to head (don't cut too deep). Use finger along spine to remove guts. Scale fish using back of knife and rinse. Cut off head, tail and fins and rinse.

Steaking
Usually for fish with high oil content.

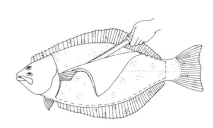

Dress fish as shown above. Cut fish in sections about one inch thick. Thick fish may require using a mallet to tap the knife through the bone. Rinse sections with water before use.

Flatfish

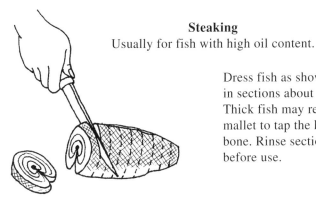

Make the first cut just behind the gills and slice down diagonally toward the head to the bone. Cut along the dorsal fin. Separate the meat from the bones by sliding the knife along the bones to the spine. Slice the meat away from the spine and continue toward the belly. Flip fish over and repeat on other side.

Sanddabs
Remove their head and the top of the pectoral fin. No need to scale or skin them. Rinse them in cold running water after cutting.

Freezing fish
Fish are best cooked fresh and will keep refrigerated up to two days. If you don't plan to eat it in that time period, you need to freeze it. Vacum packed is best or place fish in a container (plastic bag, milk carton, etc.), then fill with fresh water (helps prevent freezer burn), seal and put in freezer.

FISH COOKING

Fish with high oil content (yellowtail, tuna, barracuda etc.)are not good for frying. With any fish, regardless of how bony, always consume with caution.

Grilled Halibut

Halibut (Filleted or steaked); Mayonnaise; Herbs (Garlic, tarragon, thyme, dill, basil, sage and parsley)
Directions: Spread mayonnaise on one side of halibut and sprinkle on herbs of choice (experiment with combinations). Place on hot oiled grill, mayonnaise side down. Cook about 5 minutes on each side per inch thickness of fish (don't overcook). Turn fish and repeat on other side. Mayo will keep fish moist but not mask the flavor. Serve hot.

Pan Fried Calico Bass

Fish (filleted, cut larger fillets into smaller portions and pat dry with paper towel); Bread or cracker crumbs or cornmeal or flour (1 cup). Salt and pepper (1/2 tsp of each); Egg; Milk (1 T); Butter and oil (equal amounts).
Directions: Mix salt, pepper, egg and milk together. Dip fillet in mixture and coat with cracker crumbs. Fry fish in hot oil and butter until brown (about 2 to 3 minutes per side). Place on paper towel to remove excess oil. Serve hot with tartar sauce.

Sheephead Cocktail

Sheephead (filleted); Butter; Lemon juice; Garlic
Directions: Heat butter until clear then add lemon juice and garlic and fish and cook about 2 minutes or until fish turns white. Remove and place on paper towel. Chill in refrigerator overnight. Separate into chunks and add cocktail sauce or use in dishes similar to crab.

Fish Tacos

Fish (cut into chunks); Taco shells or corn tortillas; Toppings (cilantro, cheese, cabbage, salsa, sour cream)
Directions: cook fish chunks then dry on paper towel. Place fish in warmed taco shells and add desired toppings.

Blackened Fish

Fish (about 2 pounds of fillets); Chili powder (1 T); Black pepper (2tsp); White pepper (1 tsp); Thyme (1 tsp); Onion powder (1 tsp); Paprika (1 tsp); Cayenne pepper (1/2 tsp); 1 tsp. garlic powder; Basil (1 tsp); Lemon Wedges; Butter and oil (equal amounts).
Directions: Mix herbs together and sprinkle on fish. Fry fish in hot oil skillet. Cook until crisp on outside (about 4 to 5 minutes per side). Can be placed on hot oiled BBQ grill (5 to 7 minutes per side) instead of skillet. Best cooked outside due to smoke. Serve hot with lemon wedges and tartar sauce

Pan Fried Sanddabs

Sanddabs (Cleaned and rinsed); Garlic; Soy sauce; Salt (pinch)
Directions: pan fry them hard until their edges are crispy. The smaller bones of the fish become crispy and brittle, breaking up when chewed and the flavor of the fish is brought out fully. Do'nt eat the large bones. This fish is sweet, nut-like and moist. Also good charcoal grilled. Breaded dabs pan fry quickly in about 2 minutes per side. They're easily de-boned at the table, just like pan-sized trout or sunfish. Insert a butter knife or fork (or two) beneath the upper fillet and lift it off. The skeleton is now exposed on top of the bottom fillet. Just lift these bones off in one piece and you have a second de-boned fillet.

Tartar Sauce

Mayonnaise and sour cream (1/2 cup each); Your choice of onion, garlic, sweet pickle, green olives, capers and parsley (one diced T. of each); Lemon juice (1 tsp)
Directions: Mix all ingredients and chill about 1 hour.

Cocktail Sauce

Ketchup or chili sauce (1/2 cup); Lemon juice (2 T); Horseradish (2 tsp); Onion (1 T. diced); Worchestershire sauce (1 tsp)
Directions: Mix it all up (dash of Tabasco) and chill 1 hour.

VIII. APPENDIX

Information on emergency services, directory of local services, bibliography and index.

EMERGENCY SERVICES

On Catalina, several emergency services are available to serve the needs of boaters and divers. Primary response is provided by Baywatch Avalon or Baywatch Isthmus (Los Angeles County Fire Department Lifeguard Paramedic rescue boats). Avalon Harbor Patrol and Two Harbors Harbor Patrol will assist in emergencies. The United States Coast Guard maintains rescue boats and helicopters nearby. Diving emergencies are relayed to the Catalina Hyperbaric Chamber located at Fisherman's Cove, near the Isthmus. Medical emergencies are transfered by the City of Avalon Fire Department to the Avalon Municipal Hospital.

Emergengy at sea:

VHF may not reach local agencies from backside of the island or inside coves

If close to Avalon:	Baywatch Avalon (VHF Channel 12 or 16). Avalon Harbor Patrol (VHF Channel 12 or 16).
If close to Isthmus:	Baywatch Isthmus (VHF Channel 09 or 16). Two Harbors Harbor Patrol (VHF Channel 09).
Other areas:	United States Coast Guard (VHF Channel 16).
Emergency on land:	Dial 911

Cellular phones may transfer to the mainland. State your exact location.

Emergency telephone numbers:

Baywatch Avalon	(310) 510-0856
Baywatch Isthmus	(310) 510-0341
U.S. Coast Guard	(562) 980-4444
Sheriff Avalon	(310) 510-0174
Sheriff Isthmus	(310) 510-0872
Harbor Patrol Avalon	(310) 510-0535
Harbor Patrol Two Harbors	(310) 510-4253
Catalina Hyperbaric Chamber	(310) 510-1053
Avalon Municipal Hospital	(310) 510-0700
Divers Alert Network (DAN)	(919) 684-8111

Remember to state the type of emergency and location.

LOCAL DIRECTORY

(All addresses are in Avalon and all phone numbers are 310
area code unless otherwise noted)

Boating

Avalon Fuel Dock
Marine fuel, ice and water.   510-0046
Avalon Harbor Department Pleasure Pier.
Moorings & harbor information.   VHF 12 or 16 or 510-0535
Avalon Marine Services Pebbly Beach.
Marine repair.   VHF 16 or 510-9534
Avalon Mooring Service
Mooring & diving services.   VHF 12 or 510-0779

Catalina Conservancy Marineros 125 Claressa.
For membership information   510-2595

Marlin Club Marine Marine repair, Avalon.   VHF 16 or 510-0044
Sherrill's Marine Services Repair barge.
Marine repair, Avalon.   VHF 16 or 510-0618 or 510-1610
Two Harbors Harbor Department Isthmus Pier
Mooring information, Isthmus and outer coves.   VHF 9 or 510-4253
Vessel Assist (Boat U.S.) Towing.   VHF 16 or 800-391-4869

Diving

Catalina Conservancy Divers 125 Claressa.
For membership information   510-2595

Catalina Divers Supply Pleasure Pier.
Full service; Charter "Scuba Cat"
www.catalinadiverssupply.com   510-0330

Catalina Snorkel & SCUBA Adventures Lover's Cove
Instruction, tours & rentals   510-8558
www.catalinascubasnorkel.com

Catalina Scuba Luv 126 Catalina
Full service (nitrox); Charter "King Neptune"
www.scubaluv.biz   510-2350

Two Harbors Dive & Recreation Center Isthmus Pier
Full service; Charter "Garibaldi"
www.catalina.com/twoharbors   510-4272

Fishing

Afishinado Charters Box 1038.
Charter "Afishinado"
www.fishcatalina.com   (323) 447-4669

Avalon Seafood Pleasure Pier. Weigh-in scales and bait.   510-0197
EZ-O Ocean Charter Box 1134. Charter "EZ-O"   510-2281
Flip's Cheapo Charters Box 83.   510-1416

High Tide Traders 415 Crescent.
Fishing gear and licenses.   510-1612

Island Water Charters Box 1226   510-1707
Shamrock Charters Box 2234. Charter "Shamrock"   510-3474

Rentals

Avalon Boat Stand Pleasure Pier
  Boat, kayak, pedal boat and fishing rentals.   510-0455
Descanso Beach Ocean Sports Descanso Beach
  Kayak and snorkel rentals and tours.   510-1226
  www.kayakcatalinaisland.com
Wet Spot Avalon
  Kayak, pedal boat and snorkel rentals.   510-2229

Transportation

Catalina Express Boat service from San Pedro,
  Long Beach and Dana Point to Avalon and Two Harbors.   310-519-1212
Catalina Freight Line Pebbly Beach Rd.
  Freight service from Wilminton to Avalon.   510-0248
Catalina Passenger Service
  Boat service from Newport Beach to Avalon.   949-673-5245
Island Express Helicopter Pebbly Beach.
  Helicopter service from San Pedro and Long Beach to Avalon. 510-2525

General

Catalina Island Visitors Bureau Pleasure Pier
  Chamber of Commerce and information.   510-1520
Primitive Boat-in Camping Reservations required.   510-3577
Two Harbors Visitor Services Information.   510-4205
Two Harbors Enterprises Isthmus Pier. General information. 510-4253

BIBLIOGRAPHY

Berman, Bruce D. 1972. *Encyclopedia Of American Shipwrecks.* Mariners Press, Boston.

Dawson, E. Yale. 1972. *Seashore Plants Of Southern California.* University of California Press, Berkeley and Los Angeles.

Eschmeyer, William M. and Earl S. Herald. 1983. *A Field Guide to Pacific Coast Fishes North America.* Houghton Mifflin Co., Boston.

Gibbs, James A. 1962. *Shipwrecks Of The Pacific Coast.* 2nd Ed. Binfords and Mort, Portland.

Gotshall, Daniel W. 1981. *Pacific Coast Inshore Fishes.* 2nd Rev. Ed. Sea Challengers, Monterey.

Gotshall, Daniel W. and Laurence L. Laurent. 1979. *Pacific Coast Subtidal Marine Inverebrates,* A Fishwatcher's Guide. Sea Challengers, Monterey.

Johnson, Myrtle E. and Harry J. Snook. 1967. *Seashore Animals Of The Pacific Coast.* Dover Publications Inc., New York.

Kovach, Ron. 2002. *Saltwater Fishing in California.* Marketscope Books, Aptos.

Marshall, Don B. 1978. *California Shipwrecks.* Superior Publishing Co., Seattle.

Reish, Donald R. 1972. *Marine Life Of Southern California.* Reish, Los Alamitos.

Selected atricles, *California Diving News.* Saint Brendan, Torrance.

Selected atricles, *The log.* Duncan McIntosh Co., San Diego

INDEX

INDEX

150

INDEX

East end aerial view.

West end aerial view.